GUIDE TO THE PHANTOM
DARK AGE

GUIDE TO THE PHANTOM DARK AGE

EMMET SCOTT

Algora Publishing
New York

Library of Congress Cataloging-in-Publication Data —

Scott, Emmet.
  Guide to the phantom Dark Age / Emmet Scott.
     pages cm
  Includes bibliographical references and index.
     ISBN 978-1-62894-039-8 (soft cover: alk. paper) — ISBN 978-1-62894-040-4 (hard
cover: alk. paper) — ISBN 978-1-62894-041-1 (ebook) 1. Middle Ages. 2. History—Errors,
inventions, etc. 3. Illig, Heribert. I. Title.
     D117.S95 2014
     940.1'2—dc23
                              2013049445

Front Cover: The Enthroned Rulers by the Master of Reichenauer School

Printed in the United States

TABLE OF CONTENTS

FOREWORD

Using the most up to date mathematics as well as knowledge of celestial me-
chanics, modern astronomers can calculate very precisely where and when each
and every solar eclipse was visible over the past few thousand years. This "retrocalculation," as it is known, has placed an invaluable tool in the hands of historians. It so happens that eclipses — particularly those that were total — were of
great interest to ancient writers, who, though understanding them to be a natural phenomenon, nonetheless invested them with a quasi-religious significance.
The writings of the ancients are full of these events. From late antiquity alone,
that is, form the beginning of the first century to the end of the eighth, occidental
authors reported well over forty solar eclipses and often also included information about precisely where the phenomenon was visible.

As might be expected, modern scholars have examined these reports with
great interest. They can, after all, either confirm or refute the accuracy of the
ancient writers: Were these men trustworthy reporters of actual events, or were
they fabulators who freely indulged their imaginations? What then do the records say?

The astonishing thing is that not a single solar eclipse reported by the ancient
authors can be confirmed by modern retrocalculation! One or two come reasonably near, within half a decade or so; but the vast majority show no correlation
whatsoever between the ancient report and the modern calculation.

What, we might ask, could possibly be wrong? Were the ancient authors after
all fantasists who invented eclipses to spice up their histories? Or were they just

ignorant of the events to which they provided such precise chronological information? Modern experts have in fact resorted to both these answers in explanation. However, scholars have now also noted a curious feature of the eclipse record. If three centuries is added to the date of the ancient eclipse, as provided by the Roman (or Greek or Frankish) author, then it fits almost precisely with the modern calculation. In fifteen of the forty-odd reports the discrepancy amounts to precisely three hundred years minus forty-six days. In five, the discrepancy is three hundred and one years, and in two cases it is two hundred and ninety-nine years. In short, if we assume that the events reported by the writers of ancient Rome and Byzantium occurred three centuries closer to our own time, the eclipse record fits perfectly!

What can all this mean?

INTRODUCTION

The book that follows starts with the premise that the three centuries between roughly A.D. 615 and 915 never existed at all and are "phantom" years inserted into the calendar during the early Middle Ages. This being the case, we are not now in the year 2014, but in — or around — the year 1714.

This of course is in line with the thesis first presented by German author Heribert Illig in the early 1990s, who has, since then, published several books as well as innumerable articles and television documentaries to prove his point. I do not in these pages intend to simply reiterate what Illig has said, though a certain amount of repetition will be unavoidable. Some of the most essential evidence for the existence of this phantom time will need to be presented, especially as it is as yet so little known in the English-speaking world. It will be seen that the broad sweep of archaeological investigation over the past century has signally failed — much to the exasperation of the excavators — to produce anything substantial for the three centuries between 615 and 915. Even in sites that were occupied apparently continuously from the Roman period to the medieval (and there are very many of them), material for the three dark centuries is mysteriously missing. Even worse, the settlements of the early seventh century lie immediately underneath those from the early tenth, without any intermediate gap, and the material culture of the two epochs shows striking signs of continuity. Indeed, were historians not saddled with chronological considerations, they would have had no hesitation in proclaiming the tenth century settlements to be the direct successors to those of the seventh: Tenth century art and architecture, as expressed most eloquently in the early Romanesque, looks to all intents and purposes like the direct successor of the late Roman styles of the Merovingians and Visigoths.

The evidence of archeology proves it and so do the written sources. Everywhere there are retarded echoes, events and characters of the seventh century which reappear in the tenth century, sometimes with a minor name change. The Ural-Altaic-speaking Avars, for example, who take possession of the Hungarian Plain in the late sixth century, look very much like the Ural-Altaic-speaking Magyars who take possession of the Hungarian Plain in the late ninth century. The Langobards or Lombards, whom we find in possession of Italy in the early seventh century, seem very much like the Lombards whom we find in possession of Italy at the start of the tenth. The Frankish Merovingians of the sixth and early seventh centuries seem to reappear in the Frankish Carolingians of the ninth and tenth centuries. Even in the Islamic world we find the same phenomenon: the Muslim conquest of northern India by Mohammed bin Qasim around 710 sounds uncannily like the Muslim conquest of northern India by Mahmud (Mohammed) of Ghazni around 1010. Again, the Christian *Reconquista* of Spain against the invading Moors is said to have commenced with the victory of Don Pelayo in northern Spain around 718, but the real *Reconquista* had to wait another three centuries to materialize with the victories of Roger de Tony in 1018. It is as if history had terminated in the early seventh century, then recommenced, without any appreciable disruption or disturbance, in the early tenth.

The gap thus appears both in written history and in archeology, but often it shows itself in a combination of the two. So for example Macbeth, a Scottish king of the mid-eleventh century, was, according to tradition, besieged at Dunsinnan Castle, where he was eventually slain. Yet archaeologists, much to their surprise, could find no eleventh-century castle at the site. What they found was a late Iron Age hill fort that had been abandoned in the eighth century — almost precisely three hundred years before Macbeth was holed up in the place.

The above represents a tiny sample of the manifold evidences strongly suggesting that Heribert Illig is right and that somehow or other three hundred years that never existed have been inserted into our calendar. The first thought that occurs upon being presented with this assertion is: What could possibly have caused such a distortion? This is followed by incredulity. How, we ask ourselves, could such a mistake have occurred? Has there not been a continuous recording and chronicling of events straight from the Roman period through into the medieval? How could Christian monks and scribes, who presumably dated their years in accordance with the number that had elapsed since the birth of Christ, have been so monumentally mistaken? And what about the Islamic world: does its calendar not agree with ours? Were they then involved in some giant conspiracy to distort history, a conspiracy taking in the princes of Christendom as well as those of Islam?

These questions will be dealt with as we proceed, and it will be found that they do not present the insurmountable problem that we first imagine. We shall find, for example, that the late Roman world, contrary to popular belief, did not in fact employ the *anno domini* calendar, a system which only came into use in the eleventh century. It is true that upon converting to Christianity the Romans did begin to use the Bible as a chronological guide, but the calendar they adopted began with the Creation of the world, which the Old Testament placed anywhere between 5,500 and 4,000 years before the birth of Christ. When the Romans adopted Christianity, in the latter fourth century, believers were not very much interested in when Jesus was born; their attention was focused far more on when he would return, as he had promised. The computations of Dionysus Exiguus in the fifth/sixth century, so widely quoted nowadays, were virtually unknown in his own time.

By the first half of the seventh century, therefore, very few people had any knowledge of the number of years that had elapsed since the birth of Christ. Calendars throughout the former territories of the Western Empire tended to use varying estimates of the Year of Creation, or Age of the World, as it was called. More often than not, however, both lay and church bodies tended to date the year according to the reign of the present king or emperor. And people had concerns other than the calendar to consider, for the seventh century saw the empire embroiled in its greatest ever crisis. It is no coincidence that the beginning of the dark centuries, as defined by Gibbon and a host of later historians, occurs in the first quarter of the seventh century, coinciding precisely with the reign of Heraclius and the definitive end of classical Greco-Roman civilization. The distortion of history was inextricably linked with the great rift between the Eastern and Western Roman Empire which occurred in the latter years of Heraclius' reign. From that time onwards the Germanic rulers of the West ceased to regard themselves as functionaries of the emperor in Constantinople. This process would lead inexorably to the re-establishment of the Western Empire under a dynasty of Germanic kings, and to the break between the Latin Church of the West and the Greek Church of the East.

It was Heraclius, of course, who first came into military conflict with the Arabs, and it was in his reign that Constantinople lost Jerusalem to the Persians, in 614, a date which, according to Heribert Illig, marks the commencement of the phantom time. The military catastrophes which followed that event led within a few decades to the complete disappearance of the Eastern Empire in the Middle East and North Africa and to the closing of the Mediterranean by Saracen piracy. This latter brought about the cultural isolation of Western Europe.

The importance of Heraclius' reign as a historical watershed was recognized by Gibbon two hundred years ago. In Chapter 48 of the *Decline and Fall* he wrote: "From the time of Heraclius, the Byzantine theatre is contracted and darkened: the line of empire, which had been defined by the laws of Justinian and the arms of Belisarius, recedes on all sides from our view; the Roman name, the proper subject of our inquiries, is reduced to a narrow corner of Europe, to the lonely suburbs of Constantinople."

Darkened and contracted indeed. Gibbon relied only upon written history, but that picture of contraction and darkening has been fully confirmed by archeology, which, in the past half century, has been unable to cast any fresh light upon the next three centuries of Byzantine history. On the contrary, excavators have been astonished by the complete absence of almost all signs of life during the latter seventh, eighth, ninth, and early tenth centuries.

The same darkness manifests itself in the West. So we find for example after a period of prosperity and expansion under the Merovingian king Chlothar II (584–629), the world of Gaul too becomes clouded and dim. We are told that, "Chlothar II's son Dagobert (622–38) is often seen as the last of the great Frankish kings of the Merovingian dynasty. After him came *les rois fainéants*, the 'Do-Nothing Kings', who peter off into obscurity in the eighth century...." (Edward James, *The Franks* [Basil Blackwell, Oxford], 1988), p. 230) In the words of Sidney Painter, "If one is to call any period the 'Dark Ages,' the later Merovingian period [after Dagobert I] is the one to choose." (Sidney Painter, *A History of the Middle Ages, 284–1500* [Macmillan, 1953], p. 68)

That the Arabs wrought great destruction to the Eastern Empire at this time is beyond question, and that they may have to some extent isolated Europe culturally and economically by a blockade of the Mediterranean is also well enough understood. As early as the 1920s indeed Henri Pirenne had identified the Arabs as the authors of Europe's Dark Age. Their closure of the Mediterranean through piracy undoubtedly led to a degree of cultural impoverishment in the West, and this was probably made even more acute by the termination of papyrus supplies to Europe, a setback which can only have led to a marked decline in literacy, as well as to the loss of the great bulk of Greco-Roman literature. These things exacerbated the already backward and rural condition of Europe, a condition which had prevailed even at the height of the Roman Empire. But the Arab assault on Byzantium had another and unexpected result, as Pirenne also noted: The reduction of the Eastern Empire to Constantinople and a small region of south-east Europe freed the West immediately and dramatically from the power of their eastern neighbor; and with the decline of the Eastern Empire the latter regions commenced to detach themselves economically, politically and religiously from it. Pirenne remarked that until the arrival of the Arabs, no Germanic king of the West dared mint coins imprinted with anything other than the image of the Emperor in Constantinople; for in the century following the abolition of the Western Empire, the provinces of the West continued to be seen as part of the empire, whose capital now lay in the East. Any assertion of independence on the part of a barbarian king was liable to bring conflict with the emperor in Byzantium. The coinage minted by the Gothic and Frankish kings underlined their subservience. From the time of Chlothar II (d. 629), however, the rulers of the West commenced to impress their own images on their coins, and this was symbolic of a new-found independence. It was thus the destruction of Byzantium's power, said Pirenne, in the wake of the Arab wars, which eventually led to the re-establishment of the Western Roman Empire under Charlemagne.

The re-establishment of the Western Empire is of course generally viewed as a major watershed in the history of Europe and it signaled, as it were, the cultural and religious independence of temperate and northern Europe after centuries of domination by the Mediterranean culture represented by Rome. Why it should have occurred in the year 800, under Charlemagne, rather than about 150 years earlier, in the aftermath of Heraclius' reign, can only be seen as somewhat strange, given the fact that Byzantine power was already reduced to almost nothing by 660. Pirenne himself could not answer this question, and he never queried anything as fundamental as the chronology. Why *did* the Germanic kings wait so long before asserting their independence, when Byzantium had been powerless to stop them for a full century and a half? The answer to this, as to so many other "puzzles" and conundrums about the early Middle Ages, is finally supplied by Illig. The monarchs of the West did not wait 150 years to assert their independence: Otto I (the Great), who is said to have "revived" the Holy Roman Empire in the tenth century after it again went into abeyance in the ninth, is now seen — following Illig's system — as the Germanic king who revived the Western

Empire, not in 962, but in 662 (or to be precise 665 in Illig's chronology) — little more than a couple of decades after the rout of Byzantium by the Arabs. But in claiming the imperial crown of the West, Otto I was taking an unprecedented step: a German prince robing himself in the purple of the Caesars. What he did was unheard of, and a historical precedent would have been very useful from Otto I's point of view.

Now, it is well understood that when medieval kings and prelates needed a precedent they simply invented one. In this, Otto was no different from his contemporaries: a previous Germanic Emperor of the West was needed, so one was created — and thus was born the myth of Charlemagne.

That the "Carolingian" kings (for whom little or no archaeological evidence has been found) were much honored by Otto I and his successors is well known; yet Illig has argued in some detail that the entire Carolingian line was an invention of Otto I and Otto II. And if one is to create a fictitious German emperor, such a figure, along with his ancestors and progeny, would need two or three centuries in which to reign, and one would therefore be involved in a general distortion of chronology. That, according to Illig, is what Otto III ordered, creating an extra three centuries of history which was then inserted between Otto's epoch and the Roman age. In the "new chronology" invented by the Ottonian emperors, Otto I was not then crowned in 662, but in 962, 162 years after his supposed predecessor and ancestor Charlemagne.

Viewed in the light of Illig's chronology, Pirenne's dramatic insights finally make sense; and this is the case with European history as a whole. Indeed, the picture that emerges as soon as the phantom centuries are removed is at once astonishingly new and yet strangely familiar. Facts previously incomprehensible and even outlandish now begin to make perfect sense. For one thing, the tenth/eleventh century "Renaissance" in Europe, with its proliferation of Romanesque (or "Roman style") churches and cathedrals, reveals itself to be the natural organic development of the sixth/seventh century revival, which saw a proliferation of new churches and cathedrals, and they were built in a late Roman style. Again, we see now why the cultural impact of Islam, which we should have expected in the seventh century, is only felt in the tenth, when Europe imported a plethora of new ideas and technologies, such as the windmill, Arabic numerals, paper, and a host of other things from the Islamic world. And if the Dark Age never existed, then the West never went into a terminal decline as it entered the Christian Age. On the contrary, the revival of the Roman world under the influence of Christianity (promoting an increase in the birth rate and population in general), which had commenced so promisingly in the fifth and sixth centuries, continued into the seventh and eighth centuries, during which time Europe experienced its mini "Renaissance." All the scientific and technological innovations which characterized Europe of the tenth and eleventh centuries, actually then appeared in the seventh and eighth centuries, and these two hundred years, far from being a "Dark Age," mark an epoch of remarkable growth and rapid development; a time during which Europe finally left behind the stagnation of the late pagan Roman world.

It was during these two hundred years too that Latin and Greek civilization, in the form of the Christian religion, finally encompassed the whole of Europe. By 1050 (i.e., 750), new churches, monasteries and centers of learning were being erected as far north as Arctic Scandinavia and as far east almost as the Ural Mountains in Russia. What the Roman legions had failed to achieve in many centuries was accomplished by Christian missionaries in a few decades.

Acceptance of Illig's thesis will thus have profound consequences for our understanding of Europe's development and progress during the crucial years which followed the collapse of the Roman Empire and saw the emergence of medieval Christendom. A total rethink of Christianity's impact, for one thing, will be demanded, and the old notion of an Islamic Golden Age coexisting for centuries with a darkened and primitive Europe will have to be abandoned. Islam's epoch of economic and scientific superiority is now revealed to have been much shorter than hitherto imagined — no more than a few decades — and to have been but the final afterglow of the glories of Sassanid Persia, an afterglow which was shortly to be extinguished under the dead weight of Islamic theocracy. Even more to the point, if we remember that Islam inherited the wealthiest, most populous and most economically advanced parts of the Middle East in the seventh century, and if we remember that Europe was at that time, and had been for centuries, under the Roman Empire, an under-populated rural backwater, we can only be astonished at the rapidity of the West's rise — how quickly the Islamic world was equaled and then surpassed by the impoverished farmers and barbarians of Europe. The fact that Europe was ready by the end of the eleventh century, which we now know, thanks to Illig, was the end of the eighth, to launch a major counter-attack against Islam into the heart of the Muslim world — the Crusades — can only speak of a rapid and indeed dramatic growth of Europe's population between the fifth and eighth centuries, a growth which surely had something to do with the "revitalizing" role (as Rodney Stark put it) of Christianity in the Roman world from the fourth century onwards.

Yet acceptance of Illig's hypothesis with all its dramatic permutations seems a long way off. As might have been expected, the academic establishment has reacted negatively (to put it mildly), and a plethora of articles in the popular press and documentaries on television have sought — in the German-speaking world at least — to "warn off" the public with regard to this upstart systems analyst from Munich and his "phantom time" idea. In the English-speaking world the spokespersons of academic respectability have adopted a far more effective approach — *Totschweigetaktik*, as the Germans call it: Death by Silence. All mention of Illig's name, along with his heretical ideas, has been kept out of the popular media and academia with surprising thoroughness. Nor has the internet provided a way round this blanket censorship. The guardians of orthodoxy who police Wikipedia have described Illig's idea as a "conspiracy theory," thereby applying the tried and tested method of guilt by association. Illig is thus to be judged alongside such "historical" work as Baigent's, Leigh's and Lincoln's *Holy Blood and Holy Grail*, or even Dan Brown's *DaVinci Code*.

Illig's work is of course nothing like these. Well-known medieval forgeries, such as the Donation of Constantine and the Pseudo-Isidorean Decretals, were indeed conspiracies when they were written: the Donation of Constantine was exposed in the fifteenth century; the Pseudo-Isidorean Decretals had to wait until the nineteenth century before being exposed. The various chronicles and annals which purport to provide an accurate history of Europe during the seventh, eighth, ninth and early tenth centuries are one by one going the same way, though it seems we might have to wait a while longer before they are all exposed for the medieval fabrications that they are.

In other words, the existence of medieval conspiracies to rewrite history is well understood and denied by no one. All Illig has done is to expose another of these. It is thus hardly fair to describe his thesis as a "conspiracy theory". If the distortion of history uncovered by Illig was a conspiracy, then it was a conspiracy perpetrated once, a thousand years ago, and only then. Since that time, no one has had any idea that there was a problem.

It remains for me to emphasize that the work which follows makes no claim to being original or even very thorough. As the title suggests, I will attempt to provide the interested reader with a general guide to Illig's ideas and an overview of some of the evidence. I have, in one or two places, added a little to what Illig has already said and elaborated on proposals he made. It is evident, for example, that the primary motive for the invention of the phantom centuries was the legitimization of the Ottonian kings in their claim to the imperial purple, rather than the desire of Otto III to reign during the year beginning the millennium. It is true, as Illig said, that the final form of the invented calendar was decided by Otto III's religious fantasies, but the idea of inventing a phantom dynasty in the first place had nothing to do with religion but with legitimizing imperial pretensions.

I have spent quite a lot of time attempting a fairly detailed reconstruction of the seventh century — the century split in two by the phantom epoch. This is something Illig has generally overlooked, but is a task, I feel, which needed to be done. It is one thing to provide archaeological proof that the centuries between 614 and 914 are fictitious; it is quite another to identify precisely at which points in the seventh and tenth centuries that history ends and fiction begins.

The cut-off point between real history and phantom time is not nearly so neatly defined as might be imagined. The medieval chroniclers, who struggled to provide a "history" for the years between 614 and 914, mixed fact with fantasy, and sought, wherever they could, to use real characters and events — from both ends of the phantom period — to "fill out" the story: Thus for example the Viking invasions, which were real events of the tenth century (beginning around 950), had their starting-point back-dated into the early ninth. Again, personalities such as King Offa and King Alfred, who were near-contemporaries of the latter tenth century (flourishing around the 980s — i.e., 680s), were made to be personalities of the eighth (in the case of the former) and the mid-tenth (in the case of the latter) centuries.

Trying to untangle this web of confusion, which is absolutely essential to providing a plausible reconstruction of the "Dark Age" years, is therefore one of the tasks attempted in the pages to follow.

Aside from issues such as these, however, the ideas which follow belong to Heribert Illig and to no one else.

CHAPTER 1: THE DARK AGE

The term Dark Age, or "dark period", was first introduced into the nomenclature of historians during the fourteenth century by the Italian scholar Petrarch. The term was not originally pejorative, but reflected merely the fact that little was known of European history in the centuries between the fall of the Western Empire, an event normally dated to 476, and the beginning of the eleventh century. It seemed that few great monuments were built after the fall of Rome, though the castles and cathedrals raised by the European princes from the eleventh century onwards still adorned the landscape of the continent. These latter men presided over a real civilization, though it seemed to be a civilization of a somewhat inferior kind to that which had flourished under the Caesars. That, at least, was the general opinion in Europe by the time of the Renaissance. The philosophers they read and admired tended to be those of Greece and Rome, and the Renaissance was a period which self-consciously sought to revive the glories of the Classical Age.

With the advent of the Reformation in the sixteenth century the term "dark age" began to take on distinctly negative connotations. Protestant writers from the seventeenth century onwards would increasingly view everything between Constantine and the Reformation as a long and tedious epoch of barbarism and ignorance; and the same process was to continue during and after the Enlightenment, when men such as Voltaire and Kant saw the whole of what we now call the Middle Ages as a period of faith and thus the opposite of "enlightenment".

By the nineteenth century, however, it had become increasingly evident that it was impossible to classify everything between the end of the Western Empire and the Renaissance as a dark age. For one thing, it was found that Roman civilization did not come to an end in 476, not even in the West. The barbarian princes who had taken control of the western provinces in the fifth century were not the mindless destroyers it had once been believed. On the contrary, they adopted Roman civilization as quickly as they could and did everything in their power to uphold Roman institutions and customs. They also continued, by and large, to regard themselves as functionaries of the empire, and minted gold coins emblazoned with the image of the emperor in Constantinople. From him they accepted Roman titles and names, and proudly displayed these on their monuments. And they continued to build monuments in the Roman style. These chiefly comprised luxurious churches, but also included impressive secular buildings. The Frankish king of Gaul, Chilperic I (561–584), was said for example to have built two amphitheaters, one at Paris and another at Soissons.[1]

At the other end of the scale, the period we now call the High Middle Ages, from the eleventh or even late tenth century onwards, could no longer, in the light of archaeological and other research, be considered part of a dark age: the great cathedrals and castles of this time, which still stand in all their glory throughout Europe, revealed an advanced and in some ways astonishing civilization. It was recognized, for example, that the medieval cathedrals represented an advance on Roman architecture, and it was conceded that the Romans would have been incapable of building such structures. Indeed, in many areas of technology the Middle Ages were more advanced and sophisticated than classical Rome, and we need only cite the enormous list of technologies employed by the peoples of medieval Europe which were unknown to the Romans. These include the windmill, paper, the plow collar, the stirrup, horse shoes, new musical instruments such as the violin and bagpipe, Arabic numerals, algebra, distillation of alcohol, double and triple sailing masts on ships (for tacking into the wind), etc. (all by the eleventh century), and these were followed, in the twelfth to fifteenth centuries, by mechanical clocks, magnifying lenses, and a whole gamut of architectural innovations, as well as such epoch-making innovations as gunpowder and

---

1 Gregory of Tours, v, 17

firearms, printing, etc. In addition to this, it was found that medieval scientific knowledge was not nearly so mired in superstition and ignorance as had once been believed, and that in many areas of knowledge the Middle Ages were the equal, if not the superior, of Classical Antiquity. Such great figures of the thirteenth century as Roger Bacon and Albertus Magnus made advances in mathematics, experimented with light and the nature and properties of chemicals, and theorized on the size of the solar system.

So, everything as far as the late sixth or early seventh century was eventually re-designated Late Antiquity, whilst everything from the eleventh or even tenth century onwards was re-designated simply as the Middle Ages; and by the early twentieth century the term "Dark Age" had become generally confined to the period between the mid-seventh and mid-tenth centuries, a span of time which remained little known and from which very few architectural structures seemed to have survived. This was the period during which the Vikings were said to have rampaged around the continent, burning, looting and killing. Even documents of the time were few and far between, and what did exist seemed to imbue the period with a mythical or semi-mythical aura. The image was conveyed of a continent that had sunk into a primitive level of existence, with literature and the other civilized arts all but disappearing. The Anglo-Saxons, it was said, had even lost the art of pottery-making during these centuries, and the start they had made along the path of civilization in the late sixth century, when Augustine had landed in Kent and church-building had commenced throughout England, had gone abruptly into reverse. After a flurry of church-building in the early seventh century, the whole process was abandoned, and no new Anglo-Saxon churches appeared until the third or fourth decade of the tenth century. Indeed, the progress of archeology throughout the twentieth century seemed to show just how appropriate the term Dark Age was for this period. As the archaeological exploration of Europe was extended in the middle decades of the twentieth century, scholars were astonished by the lack of finds. It began to appear that, not only had civilization gone into reverse, but almost all signs of human life and existence had gone away entirely. Site after site could produce nothing for the three Dark Age centuries, though a settlement might produce abundant remains for the centuries preceding and following them.

How was this strange state of affairs to be explained? On the whole, it was generally concluded that the Germanic kings of the West, whilst initially making attempts to keep Roman civilization alive, finally reverted to type, as it were, and eventually let the great cities and monuments of the

Caesars fall into decay. This was the opinion, for example, of Alfons Dopsch, who, along with Henri Pirenne, was one of the first historians of the last century to emphasize the continuity between the civilization of Imperial Rome and the Germanic kingdoms which replaced it in the West. It was true, said Dopsch, that the "barbarians" did indeed try to live like Romans at the start. For a while, they actually succeeded, and the Frankish, Vandal, and Gothic kings presided over Roman-style cities and economies. Yet these did not last, and by the early seventh century all had gone to wrack and ruin.

That was one opinion, and it is an opinion still echoed in the highest ranks of academia.

There was another theory about the Dark Age which gained some prominence for a time. This was that of Dopsch's contemporary Henri Pirenne. According to the latter, the decline of Late Classical culture was swift and dramatic, and had nothing to do with the "barbarian" nature of the Germanic peoples. For Pirenne the key lay in the timetable of events. Ample proof of thriving Roman-style cities and economies could be found until the first quarter of the seventh century. After that they disappeared rapidly and completely. Above all, Pirenne found that most of the luxury products which the West had habitually imported from the East disappeared at this time. This was especially the case with papyrus, the indispensable writing material so essential for the smooth running of an urban and mercantile culture such as the Roman. All other eastern products, most deriving, like papyrus, from the Levantine countries, disappeared at the same time. What, thought Pirenne, could have terminated the Mediterranean trade so completely and rapidly? The fact that it seemed to occur in the early to mid-seventh century left only one possible answer: the Arabs.

Pirenne's major thesis, published posthumously in 1937 (*Mohammed et Charlemagne*), caused something of a stir, mainly because it went so decisively against the tide of current academic thought. For several decades prior to that date, historians had increasingly come to see the Arabs as the saviors of Late Classical civilization. They were viewed as arriving on the shores of a darkened and primitive Europe in the middle years of the seventh century. They brought with them, so it seemed, an advanced, tolerant and urbane culture, and they began the process of reacquainting the barbarous Europeans with the lost learning of the Greeks and Romans.

Pirenne's argument went contrary to this view and as such were treated with suspicion. Nonetheless, as an explanation for the Dark Age, it won several influential supporters, and may eventually have become the dominant paradigm had it not been for the fact that it had several drawbacks: First of all, the good points.

There was no question that the Arabs did a good deal of damage in the Middle East and in North Africa: large areas of the latter regions which had previously supported an intensive and productive agriculture was reduced to desert in the aftermath of the Arab conquests, due primarily to the pernicious custom of the invaders allowing their flocks of camels and goats to graze on cropland. This led to the rapid abandonment of the great Roman cities of the region which these fields had once supported. The stark skeletal remains of these metropolises still dot landscapes of the Middle East and North Africa, and they stand as eloquent testimony to the terrors brought by the Saracens in the seventh century. There was no question too that the arrival of the Arabs had an immense impact on Europe. Their pirate raids are well documented and proved by archeology, and there seems little doubt that the abandonment of Roman patterns of settlement (unprotected villas in lowland areas) and the retreat to defended hilltop strongholds throughout Mediterranean Europe during the seventh century was a direct response to the threat posed by Arab corsairs and slave-traders. That Europe's economy must have suffered in other ways is also evident: no normal trade could be conducted along the Mediterranean routes so long as these were being scoured by Arab pirates. Cities and towns, particularly ports such as Marseille which depended upon the Mediterranean trade, must have suffered. Furthermore, the Arab conquest of Spain and Sicily, together with major armed raids deep into Gaul and Italy, can only have caused a good degree of destruction and a certain amount of depopulation.

All this is a given; and yet, destructive though the Arabs may have been, they could not explain the evidence which archeology was beginning to uncover as the twentieth century progressed. Neither the Arabs nor anyone else could entirely and completely depopulate a continent for three centuries; and not even they could then cause that same continent to be repopulated three centuries later, in precisely the same towns and settlements, by communities employing precisely the same tools, ornaments and religious symbols. For that is what the archaeologists, much to their astonishment, began to find. Even worse, the complete depopulation and disappearance of settled life manifested itself also in those areas of the Middle East and North Africa conquered by the Arabs themselves. Admitting the destruction the Arabs wrought in the latter territories, not even they could have removed virtually all signs of human existence for a space of three centuries. North Africa, for example, in the aftermath of the Arab Conquest, is admitted to have endured a "dark age" which did not end till the start of the tenth century, when "new settlements" erected by the Arabs began to appear.[1] Archaeologists face a similar problem in Spain. There too the Arabs undoubtedly wrought much destruction, and the ruins of burned Visigothic towns and churches are regularly encountered. Yet here too there followed a complete abandonment and a disappearance of all signs of human life. Roger Collins, in his *Archaeological Guide to Spain*, could find only eleven structures in the whole Peninsula dating between the Arab Conquest of 711 and 911.[2] The majority of these are of doubtful provenance, and there is extremely good evidence to suggest that some at least belong in a later epoch. Contrast this with the hundreds of buildings listed by Collins of the Visigoth age, a period of time comparable to the first two centuries of the Arab occupation. Real and substantial Arab archeology only appears in Spain, as in North Africa, in the mid-tenth century. And it is the same throughout the Middle East in all territories west of the Euphrates. Typically we find extremely rich archeology of the Late Byzantine world, followed by a small handful of early Arabic finds — usually from the mid-seventh century, then a complete absence of all archeology until the early or mid-tenth century. As in Europe, the "new" settlements of the tenth century tend, however, to be built directly upon the old settlements of the seventh, and to possess a material culture strikingly similar to that of the seventh.

It is inevitable that facts such as these would eventually elicit radical solutions. The first of these, first mooted in the early twentieth century, was that of climate change or natural disaster. Several important authorities had earlier proposed a radical deterioration of the climate as an explanation for the desertification of much of the Middle East in the seventh century and the silting up of great harbors, such as that at Ephesus. Notwithstanding the fact that the contemporary Middle East has the same flora and fauna as the ancient and medieval, it was argued that some form of catastrophic change must have occurred to reduce such vast areas to desert in such a short time. But whilst a reduction of rainfall might conceivably have reduced large areas of the Middle East and North Africa to desert, what then was to blame for the depopulation of Europe at the same time? There is no question of Europe ever having been a desert or anything remotely resembling one. Such consid-

---

1 Richard Hodges and William Whitehouse, *Mohammed, Charlemagne and the Origins of Europe* (London, 1982), p. 71
2 Roger Collins, *Spain: An Oxford Archaeological Guide to Spain* (Oxford University Press, 1998)

erations led inevitably to ever more radical conclusions. It was theorized by one school of thought that a pandemic of epic proportions might have decimated the populations of Europe and the Middle East simultaneously, leaving only impoverished remnants in both areas. Another school in more recent times has gone even further and proposed some form of comet or asteroid catastrophe as an explanation. This latter idea might seem utterly fantastic, but it has to be admitted that, given the totality of the population crash which the seventh, eighth, ninth and early tenth centuries seem to have witnessed, to be arguably the more likely solution.

What Caused the Fall of Rome?

In view of such chaotic and apparently contradictory evidence it is perhaps necessary to look again at the whole question of Rome's decline and fall. This is surely central to the whole Dark Age question.

Theories about the fall of Rome have of course been thick on the ground for many centuries. As we saw above, the "traditional" view, that it had been caused by the violence of the invading barbarians in the fifth century, was seriously undermined by the application of new and more stringent methods of historical inquiry during the nineteenth century. Indeed, by the first decades of the twentieth century it had become apparent that, as an imperial power, Rome was already in a fairly advanced state of decay by the end of the second century — over two hundred years before the official "end" of the empire in 476. Historians began to speak of the "crisis" at that time. They noted a contraction of Roman power in the third century: the loss and abandonment of several provinces, beginning with Dacia and parts of Germany. They noted too a general shrinking of cities and the cessation of construction on a monumental scale. All the great structures which to this day dot Europe and elicit the admiration and astonishment of the tourist — the aqueducts, the amphitheaters and the city walls — were raised before the beginning of the third century. After that, there was almost nothing. More and more historians began to discern "a fundamental structural change" at the time, "which the great emperors at the end of that century, and Constantine himself at the beginning of the next, did but stabilize."[1] A new consensus developed, according to which there were "two successive Roman Empires.... First, there is the Roman Empire of Augustus and the Antonines, of which we mainly think, the majestic web of planned cities and straight roads, all leading to

---

1 Hugh Trevor-Roper, *The Rise of Christian Europe* (2nd. ed., London, 1966), p. 27

Rome.... Secondly, after the anarchy of the third century, there is the 'Lower Empire', the rural military empire of Diocletian and Constantine, of Julian the Apostate and Theodosius the Great. This was an empire always on the defensive, whose capital was not Rome, but wherever warring emperors kept their military headquarters: in the Rhineland, behind the Alps or in the East; in Nicomedia or Constantinople, in Trier, Milan or Ravenna."[1]

The Roman Empire, it thus became clear, was already in an advanced state of decay by the year 200; and it was also increasingly less "Roman". We hear that, "Already before the 'age of the Antonines' [in the second century] it had been discovered as Tacitus remarked that emperors could be made elsewhere than in Rome," and, as the above writer drily remarked, "By the third century AD they were generally made elsewhere." In that century, we know, "there were not only military emperors from the frontier: there were also Syrian, African and half-barbarian emperors; and their visits to Rome became rarer and rarer."[2] And the advent of "half-barbarian" emperors was paralleled by an increasingly half- or fully barbarian army. From the third and even second century historians noted the recruitment into the Roman legions not only of great numbers of "semi-barbarians" such as Gauls and Illyrians, but of actual barbarians, such as Germans and Sarmatians. Indeed, so far had this custom gone by the fourth century that by then several distinguished Roman families boasted a barbarian ancestor many generations earlier.

The crisis of the third century naturally became the subject of intense debate amongst historians. Nowadays it is often regarded as having an economic origin, and scholars talk of inflationary pressures and such like. This may be partly true; but it seems undeniable that the real problem lay deeper. There is now little dissension on the belief that by the year 150 the population of the empire had ceased to grow and had begun to contract. The inability to hold the most outlying of the provinces, in Dacia and Germany, is viewed as an infallible sign of a general shrinkage, and archeology has provided solid evidence: by around 400 the great majority of the empire's towns and cities occupied less than half the space they did in 150. There are also clear signs of a marked decline in rural populations: excavations in southern Etruria and elsewhere in Italy have shown a fairly dramatic fall in rural populations from the end of the second century through to the fifth.[3]

From the same period archaeologists have noted not only the cessation of major new building but also the demolition and recycling of existing monu-

---

1 Ibid.
2 Ibid., p. 47
3 Hodges and Whitehouse, op cit, pp. 40-42

ments.[1] There appears also in the urban settlements of temperate Europe a layer of dark humic soil, sometimes more than a meter thick, containing cultural debris — pottery, bones of butchered animals, glass fragments, etc — mixed into it, covering occupational remains of earlier centuries. "The dark earth," says one historian, "has been found to contain remains of timber-framed, wattle-and-daub huts, along with sherds of pottery and metal ornaments datable to the late Roman period. These observations demonstrate that people who were living on the site were building their houses in the traditional British [and north European] style rather than in the stone and cement fashion of elite and public Roman architecture."[2] "What are we to make of these two major changes reflected in the archaeology?" the same writer asks. He concludes that, "After a rapid growth in the latter part of the first century.... [there was] a stoppage in major public architecture and a reverse of that process, the dismantling of major stone monuments, at the same time that much of the formerly urban area seems to have reverted to a non-urban character."[3]

What could have caused such a dramatic and sustained demographic collapse? As might be expected, writers of various hues have not been slow to propose answers. These range from the plausible to the bizarre. The best explanations, however, have kept an eye both on archeology and on the written sources, and what has emerged over the past fifty years is a picture of a Roman Empire unfamiliar to most students of classical civilization. It is picture of a world immersed in decadence, squalor and brutality.

Life in a Roman city, it seems, was anything but comfortable. The image of the good life of centrally-heated villas with mosaic floors and marble pillars — the image generally presented to the public in guidebooks and documentaries — was of course far from typical. Much new research has been done on the living conditions of ordinary Romans in the last fifty years, and what has emerged is the picture of a life of almost unimaginable squalor. The cities, by modern standards, were packed: people lived in appallingly confined spaces. In Rome, the great majority of the poor inhabited multi-story apartment blocks named *insulae* ("islands"), which were little more that multi-story slums. They were also death traps. Several Roman writers noted that the most frequently heard sound in the city was the roar of collapsing *insulae*. They were constructed of the cheapest materials, and their occupi-

---

1 See e.g., Peter Wells, *Barbarians to Angels* (New York, 2008), pp. 109-10
2 Ibid., pp. 111-12
3 Ibid., p. 112

ers rarely had any warning of their impending disintegration. The streets around these *insulae* contained a central channel into which the inhabitants threw their sewage. The whole city stank, summer and winter, and so great was the stench that even the rich, in their exclusive areas, could not avoid contact with it. Hence the annual retreat in the springtime to their summer residences in the countryside.

As might be imagined, deadly epidemics were commonplace, and the failure of the ancients to understand the pathology and spread of infections led to a plethora of pandemics which wiped out millions.

Crime too was of epidemic proportions; and a society which exacted the death penalty for minor offenses offered no real deterrent against more serious crimes such as murder.

The sheer savagery of Roman attitudes is of course already well known, and we need not labor the obvious fact that people who could watch other human beings being torn to shreds by wild beasts for "entertainment" were of a very low spiritual state. The institution of slavery, by its very existence, had a corrupting effect on attitudes, and slaves, as the property of their owners, could be exploited in whichever way their owners wished. All of them, both male and female, were the sexual playthings of their masters, and must submit to the sexual demands of their owners at any time or place. The sex "industry" was a major employer, as excavations at Pompeii, Herculaneum, and numerous other ancient cities have revealed only too graphically.

As might be imagined, a society which harbored such attitudes did not shrink from taking drastic measures to deal with the unwanted issue of casual liaisons, and the practice of infanticide was widespread and commonplace in the classical world.[1] Official Roman documents and texts of every kind, from as early as the first century, stress again and again the pernicious consequences of Rome's low and apparently declining birth-rate. Attempts by the Emperor Augustus to reverse the situation were apparently unsuccessful, for a hundred years later Tacitus remarked that in spite of everything, "childlessness prevailed,"[2] whilst towards the beginning of the second century, Pliny the Younger said that he lived "in an age when even one child is thought a burden preventing the rewards of childlessness." Around the same time Plutarch noted that the poor did not bring up their children for fear that without an appropriate upbringing they would grow up badly,[3] and by the

---

1 See e.g., William V. Harris, "Child Exposure in the Roman Empire," *The Journal of Roman Studies*, Vol. 84 (1994)

2 Tacitus, Annals of Imperial Rome, iii, 25

3 Plutarch, *Moralia*, Bk. iv

middle of the second century Hierocles claimed that "most people" seemed to decline to raise their children for a not very lofty reason [but for] love of wealth and the belief that poverty is a terrible evil.[1] Efforts were made to discourage the practice, but apparently without success: the birth-rate remained stubbornly low and the overall population of the empire continued to decline.

A major and exacerbating factor in the latter was the fact that baby girls seem to have been particularly unwanted. A notorious letter, dating from the first century BC, contains an instruction from a husband to his wife to kill their newborn child if it turns out to be a girl:

> I am still in Alexandria.... I beg and plead with you to take care of our little child, and as soon as we receive wages, I will send them to you. In the meantime, if (good fortune to you!) you give birth, if it is a boy, let it live; if it is a girl, expose it.[2]

Although it may be tempting to dismiss this letter as anecdotal, the very casualness of the writer's attitude shows that what he was saying was not in any way regarded as unusual or immoral. In such circumstances we cannot doubt that girls were especially selected for termination, and since the propagation of populations is fundamentally related to the number of females, such a custom can only have had a devastating effect on the demographics.

In addition to infanticide the Romans also practiced very effective forms of birth control. Abortion too was commonplace, and caused the deaths of large numbers of women, as well as infertility in a great many others,[3] and it has become increasingly evident that the city of Rome never, at any stage in her history, had a self-sustaining population, and numbers had continuously to be replenished by new arrivals from the countryside.

In his trenchant study of Rome's social history during these centuries sociologist Rodney Stark wondered how the empire survived as long as it did, and came to the conclusion that it did so only through the continual importation of barbarians and semi-barbarians.[4] Far then from being a threat, the "barbarians" were seen as a means by which Rome might make good manpower shortages. The problem was that no sooner had the latter settled within the imperial frontiers than they adopted Roman attitudes and vices.

---

1 Stobaeus, iv, 24, 14

2 Lewis Naphtali, ed. "Papyrus Oxyrhynchus 744," *Life in Egypt Under Roman Rule* (Oxford University Press, 1985), pp. 54

3 For a discussion, see Rodney Stark, *The Rise of Christianity: A Sociologist Reconsiders History* (Harper Collins, 1996), pp. 95-128

4 Ibid., p.

Quite possibly, by the end of the first century, the only groups in the empire that were increasing by normal demographic process were the Christians and the Jews, and these two were virtually immune from the contagion of Roman attitudes.

Taking this into account, several writers over the past few decades have suggested that Rome's adoption of Christianity in the fourth century may have had, as one of its major goals, the halting of the empire's population decline. Christians had large families and were noted for their rejection of infanticide. In legalizing Christianity therefore Constantine may have hoped to reverse the population trend. He was also, to some degree, simply recognizing the inevitable.[1] By the late third century, Christians were already a majority in certain areas of the East, most notably in parts of Syria and Asia Minor, and were apparently the only group (apart from the Jews) registering an increase in many other areas. This was achieved both by conversion and by simple demographics. The Jews too, by that time, formed a significant element in the empire's population — and for the same reason: They, like their Christian cousins, abhorred the practice of infanticide and abortion. It has been estimated that by the start of the fourth century Jews formed up to one tenth of the empire's entire population. Whether or not Constantine legalized Christianity therefore, it would appear that in time the empire would have become Christian in any case.

The question for historians was: Did Constantine's surmise and gamble prove correct? Did the Christianization of the empire halt the decline? On the face of it, the answer seemed to be "No!" After all, less than a century later Rome herself was sacked, first by the Goths and then, several decades later, by the Vandals. And by 476 the Western Empire was officially dissolved. The general consensus then, for some time, has been that Christianity somehow failed to halt that demographic collapse in the West (though it is admitted that it most certainly did halt it in the East). However, by the latter years of the nineteenth century more and more evidence began to emerge, much of it from archeology, which seemed to suggest that Roman civilization did indeed experience some form of revival in the West during the fifth or at least the sixth century. Indeed, it became increasingly clear that much more of the heritage of Rome survived than had hitherto been imagined, and that Roman civilization flourished both in the East and in the West during the sixth century.

---

1 Ibid., pp. 95-128

The Revival of Classical Civilization in the Sixth Century

It has always been well-known that classical or Greco-Roman civilization did not die in the East, in the territories which would become, as we call it, the Byzantine Empire. This was evident from written history, and has always been accepted. However, with the age of archeology, a whole new body of evidence provided its own irrefutable confirmation. Not only did classical civilization fail to die in the eastern provinces, it experienced a remarkable revival there during the fifth and sixth centuries. In Anatolia, Syria, Palestine, Egypt and North Africa the fifth and sixth centuries saw an expansion of manufacture and trade and a remarkable growth of cities and rural settlement, and historians are now happy to talk of a flourishing and wealthy Late Classical civilization in the East well into the early seventh century. In the words of one prominent authority, "Archaeological evidence offers striking confirmation of the wealth of the Church [and society at large] from the fourth to the sixth centuries. All round the Mediterranean, basilicas have been found by the score. While architecturally standardized, these were quite large buildings, often a hundred feet or more in length, and were lavishly decorated with imported marble columns, carving and mosaic. In every town more and more churches were built ..." The writer quoted above continues: "more and more churches were built until about the middle of the sixth century, when this activity slackened and then ceased entirely."[1]

These words were written thirty years ago, and since then it has become apparent that there was very little slackening of building activity after the mid-sixth century: new and sometimes magnificent structures continued to be raised throughout the Byzantine lands until the first quarter of the seventh century, after which the activity did apparently cease entirely.

The opulence of the late classical cities has astonished the excavators. In Ephesus for example, during the fifth century, "many parts of the classical city were being rebuilt, and all the signs point to an immense mercantile wealth as late as 600. The best examples of this late flowering have been found in the excavations alongside the Embolos, the monumental street in the center of Ephesus, where crowded dwellings have been uncovered. Nearly all of them were lavishly decorated in the fifth or early sixth century, and their courtyards were floored with marble or mosaics."[2]

Again, "The sheer grandeur of the fifth and sixth centuries in Ephesus can be seen in the remains of the great Justinianic church of St. John. In architec-

---

1 Cyril Mango, *Byzantium: The Empire of New Rome* (London, 1980), p. 38
2 Hodges and Whitehouse, op cit., p. 61

tural and artistic terms the chroniclers led us to believe St. John was close to Sancta Sophia and San Vitale in magnificence. Its floor was covered with elaborately cut marble, and among the many paintings was one depicting Christ crowning Justinian and Theodora. No less remarkable are the many mausolea and chapels of the period centred around the grotto of the Seven Sleepers. These Early Christian funerary remains testify to the wealth of its citizens in death, complementing their lavishly decorated homes by the Embolos."[1]

Bryan Ward-Perkins, an advocate of the idea that Roman civilization perished in the barbarian invasions of the fifth century, nonetheless goes much further even than the previous authors. He remarks that "throughout almost the whole of the eastern empire, from central Greece to Egypt, the fifth and sixth centuries were a period of remarkable expansion." "We know," he continues, "that settlement not only increased in this period, but was also prosperous, because it left behind a mass of newly built rural houses, often in stone, as well as a rash of churches and monasteries across the landscape. New coins were abundant and widely diffused, and new potteries, supplying distant as well as local markets, developed on the west coast of modern Turkey, in Cyprus, and in Egypt. Furthermore, new types of amphora appeared, in which the wine and oil of the Levant and of the Aegean were transported both within the region, and outside it, even as far as Britain and the upper Danube."[2] This prosperity represented not just the late flowering of a decaying and doomed society; it represented, rather, in many ways, the very apex of Greco-Roman civilization. "If we measure 'Golden Ages'," he says, "in terms of material remains, the fifth and sixth centuries were certainly golden for most of the eastern Mediterranean, in many areas leaving archaeological traces that are more numerous and more impressive than those of the earlier Roman empire."[3]

Before moving on, it is important to note that the wealth and populousness of the East at this time is precisely what we would expect from the point of view of Rodney Stark and others, who see Christianity as a revitalizing force in the Roman world. The eastern provinces were of course Christianized long before those of the West and so would earlier have benefited from a natural increase in population. This is precisely what the archeology shows.

---

1 Ibid., p. 62
2 Bryan Ward-Perkins, *The Fall of Rome and the End of Civilization* (Oxford University Press, 2006), p. 124
3 Ibid.

None of this then sounds like the final days of a civilization that had essentially run its course and was waiting to expire, and we know that during the fifth and sixth centuries an enormous system of cultivation and terracing made great expanses of the Middle East and North Africa fertile and productive.

So much for the East, but what about the West? Here at least there can be no doubt that Roman civilization collapsed in the fifth century. After all, the Western Empire itself was formally abolished in 476 and its former provinces henceforth ruled by Germanic kings. But did this mean the end of Roman civilization in those regions? For centuries historians and commentators had thought it did; but progress of research over the past century has cast an entirely new light on the question. Indeed, it is now clear that Roman or Greco-Roman civilization survived far more completely in the West than had hitherto been realized. It is now apparent that many areas of the West, like the East, experienced a revival of population and prosperity during the fifth and sixth centuries, though not to the same extent as the East.

Spain, we know, was one of the most advanced and urbanized provinces of the Roman Empire, and it was also one of the earliest territories of the West to fully adopt Christianity. Here the Visigoths had established a powerful kingdom in the late fifth century, a kingdom which experienced a revival of Roman civilization during the sixth century. One of the most important sources from the period, the *Vitas Patrum Emeritensium*, or *Lives of the Fathers of Merida*, apparently written in the seventh century, provides a vivid description of everyday existence in the city of Merida, the provincial capital and seat of the metropolitan bishop of Lusitania in the sixth century. "The impression created by the *Lives of the Fathers of Merida*," we are told, "is that of a city [and a society] still enjoying a period of some prosperity in the sixth century..."[1] Even the Arab invaders, who arrived in Spain several decades later, were impressed by the size and opulence of the cities. Their annalists recall the appearance at the time of Seville, Cordova, Merida and Toledo; "the four capitals of Spain, founded," they tell us naively, "by Okteban [Octavian] the Caesar." Seville, above all, seems to have struck them by its wealth and its illustriousness in various ways. "It was," writes Ibn Adhari,

> ... among all the capitals of Spain the greatest, the most important, the best built and the richest in ancient monuments. Before its con-

---

1 Roger Collins, *Early Medieval Spain: Unity in Diversity, 400–1000*, (2nd ed. Macmillan, 1995), p. 88

quest by the Goths it had been the residence of the Roman gover-
nor. The Gothic kings chose Toledo for their residence; but Seville
remained the seat of the Roman adepts of sacred and profane science,
and it was there that lived the nobility of the same origin.[1]

This can hardly be described as the picture of a society in the middle of a
Dark Age! Another Arab writer, Merida, praises Seville's great bridge as well
as "magnificent palaces and churches,"[2]

The Iberian Peninsula has been much excavated over the past half century, and what has been found fully confirms the literary testimony. Archaeologists have uncovered a "wealth" of architectural remains, which "seem to
confirm" the impression created by the written sources.[3] We are told that,
"Continuity from classical antiquity into the sixth century is strikingly recorded at Merida" and various other places, and that "in Visigothic Spain
elements of physical continuity with antiquity were greater than is often
appreciated."[4] We hear, for example, that "the very distinctive style of sculpture of the sixth and seventh centuries, which seems to have spread to other
parts of western Baetica and southern Lusitania, appears to owe something
to the conscious imitation of the models of the earlier Roman past ... as well
as to the influence of contemporary Byzantium."[5] "Recent excavation," we
hear, "has shown that the urban centre of Merida did remain in use in the
Visigothic period and that, unlike some of the former towns of Roman Britain, it did not become a deserted or semi-rustic area. The principal change
lay in the way Christian buildings replaced the former secular public ones in
the city centre. Traces of what appears to be a substantial civic basilica, now
obscurely described as a triumphal arch, survive beside the site of the early
Roman forum. Adjacent to this structure was the Church of St Mary, the
Baptistery of St John and the bishop's palace. At least one other church was
built across on the other side of the forum in the sixth century."[6]

Evidence of the same type has been found in all the cities of Iberia between the fifth and seventh centuries. Quite literally hundreds of Visigothic-
period structures are known, and these can only represent a small fraction
of what once existed. One of the most outstanding examples of architecture
from the period, and one often quoted in the literature, is the seventh cen-

---

1 Cited from Louis Bertrand and Sir Charles Petrie, *The History of Spain* (2nd ed., London, 1945), p. 7
2 Ibid., pp. 17-8
3 Roger Collins, Early Medieval Spain: Unity in Divesity, 400–1000, p. 88
4 Ibid.
5 Ibid., pp. 88-9
6 Ibid., p. 90

tury church of St. John in Baños de Cerrato, Valencia, perhaps the oldest church in Spain. In Visigoth times, this was an important grain-producing region and legend has it that King Recceswinth commissioned the building of a church there when, on returning from a successful campaign against the Basques, he drank from the waters and recovered his health. The original inscription of the king, cut in the stones above the entrance, can still be discerned. Several bronze belt buckles and liturgical objects — as well as a necropolis with 58 tombs — have been discovered in the vicinity.

The impressive Gothic Cathedral at Valencia itself also has a crypt from the Visigoth era.

Again, the elegant Ermita de Santa María de Lara, at Quintanilla de Las Viñas, near Burgos, is a masterpiece of the Visigothic architectural style. Among its outstanding features is an unusual triple frieze of bas reliefs on its outer walls. Other surviving examples of Visigothic architecture are to be found in the La Rioja and Orense regions. The so-called horseshoe arch, which was to become so predominant in Moorish architecture, occurs first in these Visigothic structures and was evidently an innovation of their architects. Toledo, the capital of Spain during this period, still displays in its architecture the influence of the Visigoths. It should be noted too that, whilst the quality and quantity of new buildings in Spain declined during the last few centuries of Roman rule — as it did everywhere else — it showed a marked improvement under the later Visigoths. Everywhere we look there are signs of renewed prosperity and urban expansion. New cities were founded.[1] Reccopolis, for example, established by Leovigild in 578, was to become a major administrative and commercial center, and excavations at the site have dramatically illustrated the sheer wealth and sophistication of Visigoth society at the time. Indeed, all the indications are of an expanding population, something we would expect to have occurred earlier in Spain than in the other western provinces, owing to the region's extremely large Jewish population and to the very early conversion of the peninsula to Christianity. In Reccopolis and elsewhere we encounter again the use of carefully fashioned stone for entire buildings — a practice that had been abandoned in Spain by the fourth century. From then on cut stone was everywhere replaced by unhewn blocks in churches and palaces, with only the corner-stones — often plundered from earlier monuments — of cut stone. Yet by the early seventh

---

1   According to E. A. Thompson, there were at least four. In addition to Reccopolis, there was Victoriacum (apparently modern Vitoria); Ologicus (modern Olite); and Lugo, or Luceo. E. A. Thompson, "The Barbarian Kingdoms in Gaul and Spain," *Nottingham Mediaeval Studies*, 7 (1963), pp. 4n, 11

century Visigoth architects were again using carefully fashioned stone for entire buildings; and we should note, in passing, that these structures are far superior, technically and artistically, to their successors of the tenth century Romanesque.[1] During the latter epoch the cut stone of the Visigoths is replaced by rough, uncut stone, and the churches, generally smaller, are not nearly so richly decorated, with only very small arches and vaulting. There is all round a general impoverishment when compared to the work of the Visigoths, whose standards are only again reached around 1100.

So, we might be justified in concluding that archeology has only reinforced the impression laid down centuries ago by the chroniclers and biographers of a prosperous and cultured society under the Visigoths. We know that a silk-making industry had taken root in the peninsula during the sixth century — very shortly after the secret of silk-production was sequestered out of China during the reign of Justinian,[2] and we know that well into the seventh century there existed a lively economic intercourse between the Visigothic kingdom and the eastern Mediterranean. Evidence of every kind therefore leads to the conclusion that Spain under the Visigoths, like North Africa under the Vandals, experienced not a decline but a great revival of culture and prosperity.

When we look at Italy the survival of classical civilization into the sixth and even seventh centuries is obvious. No one who has strolled through Ravenna and perused the splendid monuments of Theodoric or Justinian, from the middle of the sixth century, can be under any illusion that Greco-Roman civilization was moribund or had disappeared in the barbarian invasions of the fifth century. These structures, especially the magnificent church of San Vitale, strike the visitor as the relics of a prosperous and expanding culture.

It is true that, after the time of Justinian, Italy went into a period of relative decline — a decline which some authors have made very much of. They point to the devastation caused by the Byzantine reconquest of the country in the 540s and the subsequent Langobard invasion in the 560s as the likely cause of a decline in the occurrence of some of the more symbolic signs of classical culture, such as the high-quality red slip ware ceramics from North Africa.[3] However, we need to remember that Italy was in many ways unique

---

1   See e.g., Heribert Illig, *Wer hat an der Uhr gedreht?* (Econ Taschenbuch Verlag, 2000), pp. 106-10

2   See e.g., Louis Bertrand and Sir Charles Petrie, op cit.

3   See e.g., Hodges and Whitehouse, pp. 33-42

in the Roman world of the fifth and sixth centuries. The city of Rome itself, which housed a vast and unproductive population during the time of the empire, began to lose its political importance in the course of the fourth century. Since the city's estimated one million souls could only be maintained by the importation into Italy of vast quantities of grain and wine from North Africa and the Middle East, the loss of Rome's importance would necessarily have implied the loss of much of this population. And sure enough, by the late sixth century the city was only a shadow of its former self. Hence we should not be surprised at some signs of shrinkage in archaeological terms at the time.

But the loss of this economically inactive population would not have adversely affected the overall economic or demographic health of the rest of Italy; and we should not therefore be surprised to find that by the late sixth century there are signs everywhere in Italy of revival and growth. There was, for example, a proliferation of new church-building. The latter is always a good gauge of an ancient community's wealth, as such communities tended to invest their disposable wealth in imposing houses of worship. By the 590s and 600s new churches begin to appear everywhere, both in the territories of the Langobards and of the Byzantines. Thus Rome alone counts six surviving seventh-century churches. These are: Sant'Agnese fuori le Mura; San Giorgio in Velabro; San Lorenzo in Miranda; Santi Luca e Martina; Santa Maria in Domnica; and Santa Maria ad Martyres. Outside of Rome the picture is similar, with new churches and civic structures continuing to appear until the second quarter of the seventh century. The Langobard queen Theodelinda (c. 570–628) was a particularly active builder who is known to have commissioned numerous churches in Lombardy and Tuscany. Amongst these we may note the celebrated Cathedral of Monza (603), as well as the first Baptistry of Florence. The famous Treasure of Monza, housed in the Cathedral, contains the Iron Crown of Lombardy and the *theca persica* enclosing a text of the Gospel of John.

On the whole, the early years of the seventh century seem to have been an extremely active and innovative epoch of Italian architecture. It was then, for example, that the campanile ("bell tower") first appeared, a remarkable and striking feature of church design.[1] Some of these, such as those at Sant'Apollinare in Ravenna, are extremely large and elaborate, complete

---

1   According to the *Encyclopaedia Britannica*, the appearance of the campanile is "variously dated from the 7th to the 10th century." Here again is that curious three-century hiatus or gap whose beginning and end seem to echo each other. *Encyclopaedia Britannica; Micropaedia*, Vol. 2 (15th ed.) "Campanile."

with arched windows at various levels. Such bell towers spread quickly throughout Europe and were the inspiration for similar structures in Gaul and the famous Round Towers in Ireland, two regions that also seemed to experience a remarkable revival of art and architecture in the late sixth and early seventh centuries.

When we turn to Gaul we find much the same picture. It is important, however, to remember that even at the height of the Roman Empire Gaul was never an urbanized society comparable to Italy. Cities and towns were built by the Romans, but they were comparatively small. In the words of Patrick J. Geary, "During the more than five centuries of Roman presence in the West, the regions of Britain, Gaul, and Germany were marginal to Roman interests.... The West boasted only one true city ... Rome."[1] The largest urban settlements were in the south, in Provence and the Rhône valley. All these had grown steadily in the first two centuries of Roman rule; and it is estimated that by the year 200 the largest Gaulish cities may have housed 50,000 people. However, everything changed in the third century, when they hastily fortified themselves against the threat of barbarian invasion. The area enclosed was small, much smaller than the total urban area of the previous centuries: 30 hectares at Bordeaux and Marseilles, 20 to 30 hectares at Rheims, 11 at Dijon, and about 8 or 9 at Paris. Thus we find Gaul, as in virtually all other areas, dramatic evidence of the population decline noted throughout the empire in the third and fourth centuries. The one exception was Trier, whose 265 hectares is explained by the fact that from early in the fourth century it became the capital of the Prefecture of Gaul.[2] We are told that, "The actual population of these cities is extremely difficult to determine."[3] One estimate has it that Marseilles, one of the largest cities of Gaul, was home at this time — the third and fourth centuries — to a mere 10,000 people. Other "cities" were much smaller. Rheims is reckoned to have had a population of around 6,000, and Châlons 900.[4] "What a contrast," says Robert Folz, "with the several hundred thousand living in Constantinople or Alexandria."[5]

The fifth century, as might be expected, saw a further decline. Urban settlements continued to exist, as the Goths and then the Franks took con-

1 Patrick J. Geary, Before France and Germany: The Creation and Transformation of the Merovingian World (Oxford University Press, 1988), pp. 8-9

2 Robert Folz, *The Coronation of Charlemagne* (Routledge and Kegan Paul, London, 1974), p. 5

3 Patrick Geary, op cit., p. 98

4 Robert Folz, op cit., p. 5

5 Ibid.

trol of the country; but from the middle of the fifth century there are major changes in the countryside, where the high-quality imported products that were one of the hallmarks of Roman civilization, become extremely scarce. Above all, there is the virtual disappearance of the fine African red slip ware which had hitherto been almost ubiquitous throughout Gaul. Small denomination coinage too, especially copper currency, either disappears or becomes extremely scarce; infallible proof, in the eyes of some commentators, of a return to an altogether more primitive form of existence.

But such a judgment betrays a fundamental misunderstanding of the situation in Gaul and northern Europe in general during the Imperial epoch. Greco-Roman civilization was only ever a veneer in those territories, all of which, even at the height of the empire, remained overwhelmingly rural. It was the presence of the legions and the administrative apparatus of the empire, and this alone, which provided these territories with the little cultural sophistication they enjoyed. It was the soldiers and ancillary staff, on salaried incomes, who injected cash into the northern regions — cash spread amongst the local populations in exchange for food, raw materials, and services of various kinds. With this hard currency, food-producing Gaulish peasants could afford some luxuries such as imported pottery. Yet there was a downside: it was the very ease with which a good living could be made from supplying foodstuffs to the Roman garrisons that hindered economic diversification and tended to keep these regions agricultural. However, the withdrawal of the legions in the fifth century, together with the imperial administration, meant that circumstances were now favorable for the development of native industries; and that is precisely what we find. Archeology indicates that from the sixth century onwards, the population decline of the third, fourth and fifth centuries is reversed; new towns and new rural settlements begin to appear; and with them come new and home-grown crafts and skills.

In the Argonne area of north-eastern France, pottery similar to the Roman *terra sigillata* continued to be made in the sixth and early seventh centuries; whilst at Mayen, in the middle Rhineland, the pottery industry established in Roman times survived and flourished through the Merovingian period and into the High Middle Ages. North of Mayen, between Bonn and Cologne, rich deposits of fine clay provided the raw material for several important pottery-producing centers in the seventh century. Large numbers of kilns and pits containing fragments of misfired pottery attest to the scale of manufacturing the villages of Badorf and Pingsdorf. "Great quantities of these ceramics in settlements throughout the Rhineland, northern continental Europe, southern Britain, and even Scandinavia show how far these fine wares were traded."[1] At the same time, we know that in southern Gaul, "traditional Mediterranean pottery of late classical design continued to be produced into the eighth century."[2]

Glass manufacture, begun in the Roman period, continued under the Franks, who even introduced new forms and techniques and who exported their products throughout northern Europe. Frankish glass did not quite reach the high quality of the best Roman glass, but it certainly was made to very high standards, and it got better and better during the course of the sixth century.[3]

Mining and metal-working flourished too, in numerous locations. Amongst these, the Runder Berg in southern Germany was among the most important. Here, in a former border region of the Roman Empire, which then formed an eastern province of the Merovingian state, a thriving metallurgical industry existed in the sixth and seventh centuries. The site is the most thoroughly investigated of about fifty hilltop settlements in this part of Europe dating from the fourth to the sixth centuries: "As at the sites on the coasts of the North Sea, Irish Sea, and Baltic Sea, crafts workers at the Runder Berg employed a range of different materials. They forged iron weapons and tools. Hammers, anvils, tongs, punches, and chisels show the variety of smithing implements they used. Bronze, much of it obtained from melting down old Roman vessels and reused belt attachments, was recast into new ornaments. Models, partly fashioned objects, and molds recovered at the Runder Berg show that ornate fibulae and belt buckles were among the special personal paraphernalia fashioned there. Silver and gold work attest to the specialized manufacture of precious ornaments for elites. Glass was being shaped into vessels and beads. Antler, bone, jet, and lead were among the other materials that these craft workers fashioned into tools and ornaments."[4]

The towns and cities established by the Romans survived into the sixth and early seventh centuries, and sometimes into the High Middle Ages. These often retained their Roman names and frequently following the street plans laid down by the original Roman architects. Indeed, from the sixth century onwards the urban settlements of Gaul and central Europe, began, for the first time since the third century, to grow: "the Merovingian bishops," we hear, "were great builders, and close to their towns they founded

---

1 Peter Wells, *Barbarians to Angels*, op cit., p. 148
2 Geary, op cit., p. 101
3 Edward James, *The Franks* (Basil Blackwell, Oxford, 1988), pp. 202-3
4 Peter Wells, op cit., p. 145

sanctuaries, which were often abbeys. These foundations soon became centres of new settlements as they opened hospices for travellers and pilgrims, and attracted men to till their soil. And so in the north, centre and west of Gaul — but, by a striking contrast, not in the south — the towns began to look like nebulae: the urban nucleus became surrounded by new centres of population which ... were in their turn surrounded by walls and so turned into fortified towns like Saint-Germain-des-Prés, near Paris, Saint-Médard de Soissons, Saint-Remi de Rheims, and many others."[1]

Thus the patterns of urban settlement did not, well into the early seventh century, differ significantly from that which pertained under the Caesars, and the archeology speaks of continuity and growth.[2] The same period was to witness an explosion of church building. Although the great majority of these have now disappeared, enough have survived to bear witness to the splendor that once was. It is estimated that altogether there were around 4,000 houses of worship in Gaul by the middle of the seventh century. In the words of one historian, "What astonishes us today is the great number of churches in Merovingian towns, few of which are thought to have had more than a few thousand inhabitants: as many as 35 churches are known or suspected from Paris, for instance."[3] Again, "the sixth and seventh centuries were clearly a great age of Gallic church-building," and "as far as the [ethnically] Frankish north-east was concerned, that process accelerated with the foundation of monasteries."[4]

From the few (generally small) Merovingian churches that survive, we know that they were heavily influenced by those of contemporary Byzantium. Indeed, it is likely many of them were executed by Greek or Italian craftsmen, for the Franks were long-standing allies of the Emperor. Several of the most opulent of these basilicas were described in detail by Gregory of Tours, and we can only regret the disappearance of these monuments — some destroyed as recently as the French Revolution — with their marble columns, stained glass windows, richly-colored mosaics, and finely-wrought statuary. Here is Gregory's take on the cathedral church of Clermont. It is, he says,

> 150 feet long and 60 feet wide across the nave and 50 feet high to the ceiling. It has a rounded apse, and on either side are elegantly made wings; the whole building is in the shape of a cross. There are

1 Folz, op cit.
2 See e.g., B. Hårdh and L. Larsson, eds., *Central Places in the Migration and Merovingian Periods* (Department of Archaeology and Ancient History, Lund, 2002)
3 Edward James, op cit., p. 151
4 Ibid.

42 windows, 70 columns and eight doors. In it one is conscious of the fear of God and of a great brightness, and those at prayer are often aware of the most sweet and aromatic odour which is being wafted towards them. Round the sanctuary it has walls which are decorated with mosaics made of many varieties of marble.[1]

Another outstanding structure was the Church of the Holy Cross and Saint Vincent, built by Childebert I in Paris. Around 1000 it was described in some detail:

It seems superfluous to describe the clever arrangement of windows, the precious marbles which support it, the gilded panels of the vault, the splendour of the walls which were covered with a sparkling gold colour and the beauty of the mosaic-covered pavements. The roof of the building is covered with gilded bronze and reflects the rays of the sun, shining so brightly that onlookers are dazzled, and call the church St. Germanus the Golden.[2]

We know that the architectural ambitions of the Merovingians did not end with church and monastery building. Great palaces once existed, and we know that Chilperic I (reigned 561–584), in true Roman fashion, built circuses in both Paris and Soissons.[3]

The revival of the late Roman world after the adoption of Christianity is nowhere better illustrated than in Britain and Ireland. Both these regions saw a veritable "renaissance" of learning and prosperity between the fifth and seventh centuries. One of them, southern Britain, had been part of the Roman Empire, but had seen Roman civilization decline and almost disappear in the years between the third and sixth centuries. Other territories, such as Scotland (Caledonia) and Ireland, which had never been part of the empire, were effectively incorporated into Latin civilization between the fifth and seventh centuries. Here Christianity took strong root and produced an astonishing flowering of culture. So striking was this in the case of Ireland that the island gained, in the sixth and seventh centuries, the reputation as the "Land of Saints and Scholars."

It is superfluous to dwell upon the wonderful civilization which appeared in the British Isles during the fifth and sixth centuries. Even southern Britain, which had been cut off from Latin culture by the barbarian invasions in the fifth century, was quickly reincorporated into the Roman world from the late sixth century onwards, when Augustine's mission arrived in Kent and com-

---

1 Gregory of Tours, ii, 16
2 Quoted from the *Vita S. Droctovie* by Jean Hubert in *L'Art Préroman* (Paris, 1938), p. 9
3 Gregory of Tours, v, 17.

menced the conversion of the Anglo-Saxons to Christianity. With this process came a major church-building program, a program which saw the erection of the first stone buildings in southern Britain since the fourth century.

The wealth of the Anglo-Saxon princes of this time has been dramatically illustrated by great numbers of archaeological finds. Perhaps the most spectacular of these was at Sutton Hoo in East Anglia (south-east England). Here excavators in 1939 discovered an immensely wealthy royal ship burial, dating from around 600, complete with some of the most astonishing artwork and jewelry ever unearthed in the British Isles. The fine quality and design of the metalwork indicated that it was the product of skilled and competent craftsmen, whilst the discovery of ten magnificent Byzantine silver bowls, together with two silver spoons, of the sixth century, are eloquent testimony to the vibrancy of trading and other cultural relations between Britain and the eastern Mediterranean at this time, supposedly the darkest of Britain's Dark Age. Sutton Hoo, according to one writer, has shown that "historians have underestimated, or at least understressed, the amount of moveable wealth that was at the disposal of a great seventh-century English king.... It is no longer possible to regard the culture of the Anglo-Saxon courts as a stunted and poverty-stricken version of the environment which surrounded the barbarian kings of larger peoples."[1] Again, says the same writer, "the discoveries greatly enlarge the range of contacts known to be possible to Englishmen of the early seventh century.... The discoveries at Sutton Hoo, like the traces of eastern influence on early English sculpture, should probably be taken as indications of peaceful, if sporadic, intercourse between England and the countries of the further Mediterranean."[2]

The new stone churches which began to appear at this time were of late Roman design, though often containing Egyptian or other Middle Eastern features. The very first was Canterbury Cathedral, whose foundations were laid by Saint Augustine in 602. The original cathedral and associated buildings has of course — with the exception of the foundations — disappeared, though a little more of the church which served Augustine's suburban monastery of Saint Peter and Saint Paul has been recovered by excavation, and fragments still survive of two adjacent churches of the same period. These have all been shown to be of Italian design.[3] From then onwards church-building spread throughout England, and from the mid-seventh century we have several fairly intact examples of Saxon churches, amongst which are:

1 Frank Stenton, *Anglo-Saxon England* (3rd ed., Oxford, 1973), p. 52
2 Ibid.
3 Ibid., p. 111

All Saints' at Brixworth in Northamptonshire; Saint Martin's, Canterbury (seventh-century nave with parts of possible earlier origin); and Saint Peter's on the Wall, at Bradwell-on-the-Sea, Essex (c. 654). Several others, reduced to their foundations, are also known. These structures, modest though they may be, bear eloquent testimony to the new expansion and growth which we have mentioned in Visigothic Spain and Merovingian Gaul during the sixth century.

The evidence therefore seems to show that thriving late classical societies existed throughout the Mediterranean world and parts of temperate Europe into the late sixth and even early seventh centuries. This was as true of the "barbarian" West as it was of the Byzantine East. If, then, the Barbarian Invasions did not destroy classical civilization in the fifth century, what did?

THE REVISIONIST REJECTION OF THE DARK AGE IDEA

From the middle of the twentieth century onwards, a new breed of "revisionist" historians emerged to challenge the very notion of a Dark Age or of the "death" of Roman civilization. This was partly prompted by the discoveries of archeology, but also by a re-examination of the documentary material and a general questioning of certain clichéd views about the Barbarians which had passed as accepted fact for such a long time. The new view was exemplified by Denys Hay when he wrote, in 1977, of "the lively centuries which we now call dark."[1] For Hay and others it had become clear that, contrary to what had been taught for many years, intellectual life did not ossify or contract between the fifth and tenth centuries; nor did the Church discourage learning or research. Indeed, in many ways it became increasingly apparent that Christianity played a revitalizing role in the Roman world, simultaneously creating a more humane environment, halting the empire's long-standing demographic decline, and encouraging literacy and learning. The knowledge of the ancients, it was now apparent, had not been lost nearly as completely as had hitherto been imagined. Documentary evidence showed a surprising familiarity among the scholastic thinkers of the early Middle Ages with an enormous body of Latin and Greek literature, including secular pagan writers, whose work it had been customary to believe was entirely lost to the West before the Renaissance. Thus for example Alcuin, the polyglot theologian of Charlemagne's court, mentioned that his library in York contained works by Aristotle, Cicero, Lucan, Pliny, Statius, Trogus Pompeius, and Virgil. In his correspondences he quotes still other classical authors, including Ovid, Horace, and Terence. Abbo of Fleury (latter tenth

---

1 Denys Hay, *Annalists and Historians* (London, 1977), p. 50

century), who served as abbot of the monastery of Fleury, demonstrates familiarity with Horace, Sallust, Terence, and Virgil. Desiderius, described as the greatest of the abbots of Monte Cassino after Benedict himself, and who became Pope Victor III in 1086, oversaw the transcription of Horace and Seneca, as well as Cicero's *De Natura Deorum* and Ovid's *Fasti.*[1] His friend Archbishop Alfano, who had also been a monk of Monte Cassino, possessed a deep knowledge of the ancient writers, frequently quoting from Apuleius, Aristotle, Cicero, Plato, Varro, and Virgil, and imitating Ovid and Horace in his verse.

Thus by the end of what is generally termed the early Middle Ages (i.e., by the tenth and eleventh centuries) we find that monasteries all over Europe were in possession of substantial libraries stacked with the works of the classical authors, and that knowledge of Greek and even Hebrew was widespread.

Nor, it became apparent, was the spirit of rational inquiry nearly as moribund as had earlier been imagined. It was noted for example that Gerbert of Aurillac, the future Pope Silvester II, had in the latter tenth century made important contributions in various fields of scientific research and was credited with the construction of the first mechanical clock. Another savant of this supposedly "dark" age had made experiments with flying machines, whilst various others had written treatises on geography, natural history and mathematics.[2] The caricatures which had for so long misled the public with regard to the Middle Ages were one by one exposed for as fictions. One of the most glaring of these was the belief that, prior to Christopher Columbus, Europeans had thought the earth was flat. The source of this particular fiction was traced by Jeffrey Burton Russell (*Inventing the Flat Earth: Columbus and Modern Historians*) to several anti-Christian writers of the nineteenth and early twentieth centuries, most importantly Washington Irving, John Draper and Andrew White.[3] In the above volume Russell shows in detail that writers even of the darkest epoch of the "Dark Age" had an extremely good idea of the earth's shape and of its size — thanks to the calculations of Eratosthenes in the third century BC, which they were well aware of. Science and learning, as Edward Grant as well as many other writers found, was

---

1 Cited from Charles Montalembert, *The Monks of the West: From St. Benedict to St. Bernard.* Vol. 5, (London, 1896), p. 146

2 Stanley L. Jaki, "Medieval Creativity in Science and Technology," in *Patterns and Principles and Other Essays* (Intercollegiate Studies Institute, Bryn Mawr, Pennsylvania, 1995), p. 81

3 Jeffrey Burton Russell, Inventing the Flat Earth: Columbus and Modern Historians (1991)

actually encouraged by the Church, and the old view of the Christian faith acting as a dampener of scientific inquiry had to be abandoned.[1]

Archeology too began, in some respects at least, to show an astonishing continuity between the world of late antiquity and the Middle Ages. Thus it was noted that Merovingian architecture in Gaul during the sixth and early seventh centuries bore a striking resemblance to the Romanesque architecture of France during the tenth and eleventh centuries.[2] It was very clear that there existed a direct line of connection between the two, which formed part of a single artistic and technical tradition. Again, artwork of the Ottonian epoch, in the tenth century, looked precisely like that of the seventh, or even sixth; so alike indeed are the products of the two periods that it would be impossible to tell which they belonged to without accompanying inscriptions. A seminal work was that of Peter Brown, whose *The Making of Late Antiquity* (1978) offered a new paradigm of understanding the changes of the time and challenged the post-Gibbon view of a stale and ossified late classical culture in favor of a vibrant and dynamic civilization.

In recent decades, then, quite literally dozens of authors have nailed their colors to the mast and published work decrying the very existence of a Dark Age. So prominent has this school become that it has now, to some degree at least, the default position; and to talk of a Dark Age is, in many quarters at least, to invite scorn. These writers have emphasized, in a thousand publications, how archeology has demonstrated the existence of prosperous and demographically expanding societies throughout Europe during the sixth and seventh centuries. These were, in part at least, heavily under the influence of Rome and Byzantium; though they were also heavily "native" in their inspiration. The astonishing culture that appeared in Ireland and Britain during these centuries, with its dramatic "Hiberno-Saxon" art, was surely not the signature, these writers hold, of a decadent and dying society. Architecture in stone too, throughout the former territories of the Western Empire, which had all but disappeared by the fifth century, reappeared in the sixth and seventh centuries, even in places like Anglo-Saxon England, where the Germanic migrations had effaced Roman civilization in a most thorough way. And this architecture looked distinctly Roman in appearance.

1 See e.g., Edward Grant, *God and Reason in the Middle Ages* (Cambridge, 2001)
2 V. I. Atroshenko and Judith Collins, *The Origins of the Romanesque* (Lund Humphries, London, 1985)

Early Romanesque architecture. Typical Romanesque architectural forms of the fifth and sixth centuries, showing clear continuity with the architecture of the tenth and eleventh centuries.

Fig. 1 A. Early Spanish Romanesque. Church of Santa Maria del Naranco, **mid-ninth century.** The design of the church, originally constructed as a palace, is typically late Roman and is almost indistinguishable from architecture of the sixth century. Photo by Alberto Imedio, at http://en.wikipedia.org/wiki/File:Santa_Maria_del_Naranco_2_crop.JPG. Licensed under the Creative Commons Attribution-Share Alike.

Fig. 1 B. Nave of the abbey church St. Foy, Conques, France, **1050 to 1120.** Photo accessed at http://en.wikipedia.org/wiki/File:Vo%C3%BBte_en_berceau_Conques.JPG. Licensed under the Creative Commons Attribution-Share Alike.

Fig. 1 C. Abbaye de Lessay, France, c.1056. Photo accessed at http:// en.wikipedia.org/wiki/File:LessayAbbaye3.JPG. Public domain.

Continuity too is seen in the survival of Latin as the language of learning and of the Church.

So overwhelming and striking has been the evidence for the survival of classical culture that by 1996 Glen W. Bowerstock could write of "The Vanishing Paradigm of the Fall of Rome." Bowerstock went through the archaeological evidence in detail and came to the conclusion that Roman civilization (and even in some aspects the Roman Empire) never really fell at all, but simply evolved into the culture we now call "medieval," a culture which was, however, much more "Roman" than has until recently been admitted or realized.[1] More recently, a plethora of publications, many of which look in some depth at the archeology, have argued passionately in the same vein, and we may cite Peter S. Wells' *Barbarians to Angels* (New York, 2008), Chris Wickham's, *The Inheritance of Rome: Illuminating the Dark Ages 400–1000* (2009); and Ken Dark's *Britain and the End of the Roman Empire* (Stroud, 2001), as among the most influential of these, in the English-speaking world at least.

---

1 Glen W. Bowerstock, "The Vanishing Paradigm of the Fall of Rome," *Bulletin of the American Academy of Arts and Sciences*, Vol. 49, No.8 (May, 1996)

Fig. 2 A. Ottonian (tenth-century) book-covers, showing celebration of the Mass. The artwork is indistinguishable from that of the sixth/seventh century.

Fig. 2 B. Another tenth-century book cover, showing Saint Gregory and scribes. (after K. Clark). The artistic style of portrayal and the background architecture all look typically late Roman, and could equally well be dated to the sixth or seventh century.

Fig. 2 C.
Otto III as
Christian
Roman
Emperor,
enthroned
in a Roman-
style palace.
Tenth
century.

Denying the very existence of a Dark Age, the "Revisionists" have always tended to ignore or downplay the somewhat embarrassing shortage of archeology in the roughly three centuries stretching from the first quarter of the seventh to the first quarter of the tenth. For shortage there is — as we shall shortly see — and it is the lack of material remains for these years that has prompted a general refusal to go the whole distance with the Revisionists and to write the Dark Age out of the textbooks completely. After all, how can historians be expected to ignore the fact that Europe seemed to have produced almost nothing, either pottery, coins or artifacts of any kind, for three centuries?

The archaeological hiatus stretching between the seventh and tenth centuries has provided the Revisionists' opponents with ample ammunition and has emboldened some of them to attempt a complete return to the old notion of a barbarian-induced Dark Age commencing in the fifth century. This was the stance taken in 2005 by Bryan Ward-Perkins, whose *The Fall of Rome and the End of Civilization*, reiterated a more or less traditional view of late antiquity.

Before we look at the archaeological hiatus, we should mention the thesis proposed by Henri Pirenne, who in the 1920s began to argue that the Dark Age, the real Dark Age of the seventh to tenth centuries, was inaugurated by the Arabs. The evidence, as Pirenne was at pains to show in his posthumously published *Mohammed et Charlemagne* (1938) seemed incontrovertible. From the mid-seventh century, trade between the ancient centers of high culture in the Levant and the West apparently came to an abrupt halt. Luxury items originating in the eastern Mediterranean, which are mentioned routinely in the literature until the end of the sixth century, disappear completely by the mid-seventh century, at the latest. The flow of gold, which the West derived from the East, seemed to have dried up. Gold coinage disappeared, and with it went the towns and urban settlements of Italy, Gaul and Spain. Documents of the period made it very clear that these, especially the ports, owed their wealth to the Mediterranean trade. Worst of all, perhaps, from the perspective of culture and learning, the importation of papyrus from Egypt seemed to have entirely ceased. Pirenne stressed that fact that this material, which had been shipped into Western Europe in vast quantities since the time of the Roman Republic, was absolutely essential for a thousand purposes in a literate and mercantile civilization; and the ending of the supply would have had an immediate and catastrophic effect on levels of literacy. These must have dropped, almost overnight, to levels perhaps equivalent to those in pre-Roman times.

Pirenne held that the disappearance of such Levantine products in the middle of the seventh century pointed to only one possible conclusion: that the Arabs, whose well-known predilection for piracy has been documented for centuries, must have, through their raiding and freebooting, effectively terminated all trade in the Mediterranean, thus isolating western Europe both intellectually and economically.

This is not the place for a detailed examination of Pirenne's thesis, but we should note that even if we agree with his evaluation of the impact of the Arabs — namely that they were incredibly destructive — and that it was they who effectively ended the old classical or "Mediterranean" civilization (especially in the Levant), we still have to wonder whether this could explain the complete disappearance of almost all archeology throughout Europe and the Middle East for about three centuries. For that is precisely what excavators, much to their astonishment, have found.

CHAPTER 2: THE ARCHAEOLOGICAL PROBLEM

The true scale of the Dark Age problem for historians is only grasped when we take a broad look at the findings of archaeologists over the past century. The picture that emerges is that of an apparently complete and total disappearance of all settlement and signs of human occupation throughout the continent for a period of three hundred years. This absence is evident as soon as we dig beneath the surface, but it is also apparent to the casual observer or tourist, who sees only the monuments which survive above the ground.

It quickly becomes clear to anyone who has ever visited the historic sites of Europe that, aside from the monuments of the Romans, the earliest works of architecture belong to the eleventh or late tenth centuries. If one visits the great cathedrals of England, France or Germany, one typically finds a Gothic or perhaps Romanesque structure of the eleventh to thirteenth centuries. Tourist information literature generally reveals that the cathedral was first established in the sixth or early seventh century (the case for example at Canterbury, Cologne, and a host of others), but that this early structure was demolished and rebuilt in the tenth, eleventh and twelfth centuries. Occasionally, a small part of the sixth/seventh century building may survive, in the form of a crypt, or simply as foundations. In several parts of Europe entire churches of the sixth and seventh centuries are indeed extant. In Rome for example there are perhaps five or six dating from the early seventh century. In England, building in stone entirely disappeared following the withdrawal of the Roman legions around 406, but the art was revived with the arrival of Augustine's mission to Kent in 596. Canterbury cathedral itself was established in 597, from which time onwards there was a spurt of church-building which appears to have lasted until the middle of the seventh century. From the latter period we have several fairly intact examples of Saxon churches, amongst which are: All Saints' at Brixworth in Northamptonshire; Saint Martin's, Canterbury (seventh century nave with parts of possible earlier origin); and Saint Peter's on the Wall, at Bradwell-on-the-Sea, Essex (c. 654). Several others, reduced to their foundations, are also known. After that, however, there is nothing until the third decade of the tenth century.[1] The remains of the seventh century churches invariably lie underneath those of the tenth and eleventh centuries which replaced them. Yet these churches did actually exist, whereas almost none at all were established during the intervening three centuries. And this is the pattern throughout Europe.

Castles and fortified sites present a similar picture. The classic medieval castle is said to have developed from fortified hilltop settlements which replaced the scattered lowland farms and villas of the Roman Age during the early seventh century. Many of these hilltop strongholds are known in Italy and also throughout southern France, as well as in various parts of the Aegean region and Asia Minor. But although castle-building began in these regions in the seventh century, none of the structures built at that time has survived into the modern age. Invariably, the seventh century fortresses were replaced by greater and larger edifices in the tenth and (more especially) eleventh centuries, and it is these which we see today. The tenth and eleventh century fortresses were built directly on the seventh century foundations, with nothing of the eighth or ninth centuries intervening. Even stranger, we find that, whilst the age of castle-building commenced in southern Europe during the seventh century, it only began in northern Europe in the tenth. And what is even worse, the boundary between the two ages of castle-building is often no more than a few kilometers apart. Thus for example the first fortified hilltop sites on the southern coast of France appear in the seventh century, whilst just a few kilometers away, in the Pyrenean foothills, the first castles appear in the tenth century. This is the case, for example, at Lourdes, where the fortified stronghold was clearly designed to guard the Pyrenean passes against Muslim raids in the tenth century; yet

---

1 The single exception is said to be Saint Wystan's church at Repton in Derbyshire, which contains a small crypt, dated from the mid-eight century, and chancel walls, supposedly dating from the ninth century.

just a few kilometers to the west, at Montségur, a fortified stronghold also designed to guard against Muslim raids is dated to the seventh century.

When we come to examine ordinary towns and villages, as opposed to important monuments, we find a similar pattern. Numerous cities as well as towns and villages appear to have been occupied continuously from the Roman period right through to the Middle Ages and beyond. This is demonstrated in a thousand ways, not least by the retention of street patterns and land uses of the Roman period into the medieval. In most cases, the Roman name of the city or town was also retained. Thus London was the Roman *Londinium*, Paris was the Roman *Paris*, Regensburg was the Roman *Castra Regina*, Cologne was the Roman *Colonia Agrippina*, etc. Invariably, these and numerous other cities reveal rich archeology dating from the fourth, fifth, sixth, and early seventh centuries. There are also rich remains from the mid-tenth, eleventh, twelfth centuries, etc. There is, however, as a general rule, an almost complete and astonishing gap between the early-seventh and early tenth centuries.

Such is the case, for example, at numerous excavated sites in France and western Germany, the old Merovingian and Carolingian realms. Major centers like Paris, Lyon, Bordeaux, Toulon, Trier, and Cologne display substantial material from the sixth century and up until the end of the reign of Chlothar II (584–629). But after that time there is virtually nothing. In the words of Sidney Painter, "If one is to call any period the 'Dark Ages,' the later Merovingian period [after Chlothar II] is the one to choose."[1] The depressing lack of material elicited the following comment in 1982 from archaeologists Richard Hodges and William Whitehouse, "For two decades urban archaeologists have doggedly searched for traces of seventh- to ninth-century occupation above Roman levels, simply to verify isolated historical references to the existence of an *urbs* or a *municipium*. Thwarted by the absence of early medieval deposits, there is the constant temptation to attribute tenth-century layers to the ninth century and so to recover at least something in the bid to prove urban continuity."[2] As the authors note, repeated attempts to discover any trace of urban life for these years have resulted in complete failure: "all these efforts," they remark, "provide us with an invaluable body of *negative* evidence against the continuity of towns after 600, and the case for discontinuity of urban life is very strong indeed."[3] Cologne, for example, later one of the great medieval centers, was a virtual ruin by around 700. In the words of

---

1 Sidney Painter, *A History of the Middle Ages, 284-1500* (Macmillan, 1953), p. 68
2 Hodges and Whitehouse, op cit., p. 84
3 Ibid.

one writer, "Cologne seems to have reached the nadir of its civil development during the 8th century. Only with the Ottonian period [mid-tenth century] is the town re-established ..."[1]

Vast stretches of the continent have revealed the same pattern, notwithstanding the resistance of scholars to admit as much. Until recently, for example, Austrian Professor Ferdinand Opll held that in Vienna a small community had continued to exist throughout the seventh to tenth centuries, but in August 2010 he finally admitted: "For more than 300 years [between around 610 and 910], old Vindobona [Vienna] was deserted ... Wolves were searching the ruins for prey."[2] Professor Karl Brunner of the same department has for years insisted that the entire Danube valley between Linz and Vienna was uninhabitable for three centuries.

This of course was not what excavators had expected. According to the medieval chronicles which purport to document the late seventh, eighth, ninth and early tenth centuries, there were numerous and prosperous Merovingian and Carolingian cities throughout present-day France and Germany in these years.

Everywhere archaeologists have looked they have encountered this gap; and everywhere it is approximately three centuries long. One curious feature we should note, however, is that the gap is not always — apparently — encountered precisely between the early seventh and early tenth centuries. In some areas it seems to correspond with the Merovingian epoch, leaving a gap between the final part of the Roman Age — roughly A.D. 450 — and the beginning of the Carolingian Age — roughly A.D. 750. This was the case, for example, at Dorestad, an important trading center in the Netherlands. In the words of W. J. H. Verwers, "Sand-dredgers [at Dorestad] brought up Roman and Carolingian finds ... among them three Roman helmets.... Unfortunately Merovingian material [of the fifth to eighth centuries] was not represented among the finds ..."[3] Some Carolingian cities, such as Duisburg in Germany, were only established in the eighth century and did not exist before that time.[4]

---

1 Walter Janssen, "The rebirth of towns in the Rhineland," in Richard Hodges and Brian Hobley (eds.) *The Rebirth of Towns in the West, AD 750 to 1050* (Council for British Archaeology, 1988), p. 50

2 H. Lackner, "Multikulti in Ur-Wien. Archäologie. Historiker schreiben die Geschichte Wiens neu: Anders also bisher angenommen, war die Stadt zu Beginn des Mittelalters 300 Jahre lang eine menschenleere Ruinenlandschaft," in *Profil*, Wien (2010), p. 31

3 W. J. H. Verwers, "Dorestad: a Carolingian town?" in Richard Hodges and Brian Hobley (eds.) op cit., p. 52

4 Walter Janssen, loc cit., p. 51

So, the Dark Age hiatus or period of abandonment and non-occupation occurs everywhere, but it is not always in the same place: on some occasions it corresponds with the Carolingian Age, on others with the Merovingian period. Everywhere, however, it is about three centuries long. The same phenomenon occurs outside the ancient Frankish realms, as for example in Britain, where, to complicate matters further, the hiatus frequently occurs at two different periods, which taken together add up to around three hundred years.

In Britain, as in other areas of western Europe, documentary evidence suggests a fairly uninterrupted continuation of urban settlement, with many of the Roman cities — as for example London, Canterbury, York, Leicester, Chester, etc. — retaining their Roman names; this in spite of the fact that the native Romano-British population was largely replaced by an in-coming barbarian one in the fifth century. Chronicles dealing with the ninth and tenth centuries speak of London as a thriving and populous city. What was found by excavators, however, was quite different. According to archaeologist James Campbell, "The fate of Britain's Roman cities is everywhere mysterious."[1] In every settlement, without exception, around three hundred years of the town's history was unaccounted for in the excavation record. Normally there is ample material for the period until the early seventh century, then a gap lasting three hundred years, followed by a resumption of occupation in the early or middle tenth century. On occasion, however, the gap is not continuous, but broken into two segments. This is the case, for example, in London. Here there is evidence of a prosperous settlement as far as the mid-fifth century (457), then a gap until the latter seventh century (674). After this there seems to have been continual settlement until around 850, followed by a second hiatus reaching as far as 950. Altogether, around 320 years of the city's history are unaccounted for in the archaeological record.[2]

The same situation is encountered in Chester. In the words of archaeologist A. T. Thacker: "it must be admitted that the archaeological evidence for this period [the Dark Age] is minimal. Indeed we have little evidence of any kind about what, if anything, was going on at Chester from the 5th to the 9th centuries."[3]

---

1 James Campbell, *The Anglo-Saxons* (Harmondsworth, London, 1982), p. 39
2 Hans-Ulrich Niemitz, "Archäologie und Kontinuität. Gab es Städte zwischen Spätantike und Mittelalter?" *Zeitensprünge* IV (1992, No. 3), p. 55
3 A. T. Thacker, "Early medieval Chester: the historical background," in Richard Hodges and Brian Hobley, op cit., p. 119

Thus the archaeologists find universally an occupation gap roughly three centuries long, a gap occurring, at various stages, between the fifth and tenth centuries. Yet the Dark Age chronicles, of which there are many, report thriving settlements all throughout this period, and make no mention (except on rare occasions) of abandonment. Many of the early medieval cities, it is claimed, were looted and burned by Viking raiders in the ninth century. Thus Aachen and Cologne were said to have been burned in 881, Trier in 882 and Paris in 885. However, not only have no traces of these destructions been found, we hear that there is "not the slightest [archaeological] evidence" for any such violent destruction at the time.[1]

The Vikings themselves present major problems for conventional history. On the one hand their raids are viewed as a response to the Muslim demand for white-skinned slaves and eunuchs; on the other, however, they are said to have commenced their raiding and pillaging only shortly before 800 — a full century and a half after the Muslim conquest of the Middle East and North Africa. Or that, at least, has been the received wisdom until recently. However, evidence has now emerged to show that the Swedish Vikings were indeed active in supplying slaves to the Caliphs in the seventh century: the Scandinavian trading-post of Staraja Ladoga, in north-western Russia, has been reliably dated to the mid-seventh century.[2] In addition, several Viking hoards, located throughout Scandinavia and elsewhere, contained Islamic coins of the mid-seventh century.[3]

At the other end of the Viking world, in Iceland, a similar problem has appeared. According to conventional ideas, the first Norwegian settlers arrived in Iceland in the late ninth century, when Ingolfur Arnarson led an expedition to the island. Strangely, however, the homesteads of the earliest settlers have been shown to share many features with those of the Merovingian age of the seventh century.[4]

---

1 Illig, op cit., p. 98

2 See H. Clarke and B. Ambrosiani, *Towns in the Viking Age* (St. Martin's Press, New York, 1995)

3 In 1999 a hoard found at Gotland in Sweden included "Arabic coins from the Sassanidian dynasty from the mid-7th century ..." Ola Korpås, Per Wideström and Jonas Ström, "The recently found hoards from Spillings farm on Gotland, Sweden," *Viking Heritage Magazine*, 4 (2000)

4 Excavations carried out by Margarét Hermanns-Auðardóttir. "Islands Tidiga Bosättning. Umeå Universitel. Studie med utgångspunkti merovingertida – vikingatida gårdslämningar; Herjólfsdalur, Westmannaeyjar, Island." Cited from Illig, op cit.

So, we now have the astonishing fact that in some parts of Europe events which should have occurred in the Carolingian Age (eighth to tenth century) seem actually to have begun in the Merovingian Age (fifth to eighth century), whereas in other parts of the continent events and settlements which logic would suggest belong to the Merovingian Age have in fact produced no Merovingian but only Carolingian material. In addition, we have seen that everywhere in Europe the Dark Age occupation hiatus occurs either in the Merovingian or the Carolingian strata; either the Merovingian material is missing, or the Carolingian material makes no appearance. There is not a single archaeological site which can produce finds for the entire Merovingian and Carolingian epochs, and everywhere the gap — wherever it is encountered — is about three centuries long.

We might also remark that the non-appearance of the early Merovingian age (from Clovis in 466 to Clothair II in 629) in some excavations seems very strange, in view of the fact that — as we saw in the previous chapter — this part of the Merovingian epoch was one of revival and increasing prosperity after centuries of decline under the later Romans. Why then should the early Merovingian Age, in some regions, appear to have marked the very nadir of the Dark Age?

Without going into details of this question here, it should be stressed that frequently material which one scholar might refer to as "Carolingian" is described by another as "Merovingian" — and even, on occasion — "Ottonian." And indeed examination reveals that usually there is little or no difference observable in the material culture of these three epochs which are nevertheless believed to stretch over a period of four centuries. Indeed, the tenth century artwork of the Ottonians looks in many ways astonishingly Roman and would, were it not for the discovery of an inscription linking it to the reigns of Otto I, II, or III, be dated to the seventh or even sixth century. And the confusion of the experts with regard to the Carolingians and Merovingians is even more understandable when we consider that the Carolingian kings of the eighth and ninth centuries bore typically Merovingian names. Thus the two most common of the Carolingian names, Louis and Lothair, are but modifications of the Merovingian names Clovis and Clothair. The Carolingian names have simply dropped the initial "c." Even more to the point, both sets of names have a huge number of variants, which were all in common use. Thus Clothair could also be written as Chlotar, Clothar, Clotaire, Chlotochar, or Hlothar, whilst Clovis also appears as Chlodwig or Chlodwech, whilst Louis (Lovis) is also written as Ludovic. And it needs furthermore to be stressed that no European language possessed a standardized system of spelling before the Modern age (none existed in English, for example, under after Dr. Johnson published his dictionary in the latter eighteenth century). In such circumstances, we must expect that the names of kings could have been written quite differently in different parts of their realms — leading to utter confusion on the part of modern scholars. This being the case, I would tentatively suggest that in those settlements such as Dorestad, where no Merovingian and only Carolingian material was found, the excavators have mistaken Merovingian remains for Carolingian; and following from this the real Dark Age gap occurs precisely in the three centuries between circa 625 and 925 — the late Merovingian and early Carolinian Age.

It should be pointed out here that even the major Carolingian monuments, such as for example Charlemagne's famous chapel at Aachen — supposedly built around 800 — have, upon closer inspection, been shown to date from other ages entirely, and the entire corpus of Carolingian art and material remains from before 925 evaporates as soon as it is put under the lens of detailed scholarly examination. Thus with regard to the Aachen chapel dozens of architectural and stylistic features reveal that it could not have been built before the mid-eleventh century.[1]

The confusion of Merovingians with Carolingians is not insignificant, and it is a topic we shall return to at a later stage.

The progress of excavation has, therefore, in spite of one or two complications, powerfully reinforced the negative evidence mentioned above by Hodges and Whitehouse in the 1980s, and as every new site is examined, it becomes increasingly less likely that we will ever find much from the truly "dark" centuries which seem to stretch from the first quarter of the seventh century to the first quarter of the tenth — roughly from the end of the reign of Clothair II in 629 until the time of Louis IV, whose reign began in 936.

THE ARCHAEOLOGICAL HIATUS IN BYZANTIUM AND THE ISLAMIC WORLD

Whatever might be said about Europe during the "dark age" centuries, historians did not expect to find the same decline in Byzantium and the Arab world. After all, neither of these regions had been overrun by the rude barbarians of Germany and Scythia. Byzantium in particular, capital of the eastern Roman Empire, was surely a bastion of power, prosperity and glory after the fall of the West to the tribal invaders. Or that, at least, was the opinion generally held until quite recently. As late as 1953 historian Sidney Painter was able to describe the eighth, ninth and tenth centuries at Byzantium as

---

1 See esp. Heribert Illig, *Das erfundene Mittelalter* (Ullstein, Berlin, 2005)

"three centuries of glory," and remarked that during this time, "The Byzantine Empire was the richest state in Europe, the strongest military power, and by far the most cultivated."[1] We are further informed that, "During these three centuries while Western Europe was a land of partly tamed barbarians, the Byzantine Empire was a highly civilized state where a most felicitous merger of Christianity and Hellenism produced a fascinating culture."[2]

But what a difference a few decades of archaeological research makes! In stark contrast to the above rose-tinted picture, excavators have uncovered a scene of devastation, abandonment, and poverty.

In the words of Byzantine historian Cyril Mango, "One can hardly over-estimate the catastrophic break that occurred [in Byzantium] in the seventh century. Anyone who reads the narrative of events will not fail to be struck by the calamities that befell the Empire, starting with the Persian invasion at the very beginning of the century and going on to the Arab expansion some thirty years later — a series of reverses that deprived the Empire of some of its most prosperous provinces, namely, Syria, Palestine, Egypt and, later, North Africa — and so reduced it to less than half its former size both in area and in population. But a reading of the narrative sources gives only a faint idea of the profound transformation that accompanied these events.... It marked for the Byzantine lands the end of a way of life — the urban civilization of Antiquity — and the beginning of a very different and distinctly medieval world."[3] But the world of Byzantium from the mid-seventh century was not merely "medieval," it seems to have been an uninhabited wasteland. Mango remarks on the virtual abandonment of the Byzantine cities after the mid-seventh century. The archaeology of these settlements, we hear, usually reveals "a dramatic rupture in the seventh century, sometimes in the form of virtual abandonment."[4]

The "dramatic rupture" of the seventh century is not simply another chapter of the Eastern Empire's past; it is, in Mango's words, "the central event" of her history.

So great was the depopulation that even bronze coinage, the everyday lubricant of commercial life, disappeared. According to Mango, "In sites that have been systematically excavated, such as Athens, Corinth, Sardis and others, it has been ascertained that bronze coinage, the small change used for everyday transactions, was plentiful throughout the sixth century and (de-

---

1 Sidney Painter, op cit., p. 35
2 Ibid.
3 Cyril Mango, op cit., p. 4
4 Ibid., p. 8

pending on local circumstances) until sometime in the seventh, after which it almost disappeared, then showed a slight increase in the ninth, and did not become abundant again until the latter part of the tenth."[1] Yet even the statement that some coins appeared in the ninth century has to be treated with caution. Mango notes that at Sardis the period between 491 and 616 is represented by 1,011 bronze coins, the rest of the seventh century by about 90, "and the eighth and ninth centuries combined by no more than 9."[2] And, "similar results have been obtained from nearly all provincial Byzantine cities." Even such paltry samples as have survived from the eighth and ninth centuries (nine) are usually of questionable provenance, a fact noted by Mango himself, who remarked that often, upon closer inspection, these turn out to originate either from before the dark age or after it.

The same picture of abandonment and depopulation is presented throughout the Islamic world. In fact, the entire Middle East and North Africa is a virtual blank for roughly three centuries. Normally, we see one or two finds attributed to the seventh century (or occasionally to the eighth century), then nothing for three centuries, then a resumption of archaeological material in the mid- or late-tenth century. Take for example Egypt. Egypt was the largest and most populous Islamic territory during the Early Middle Ages. The Muslim conquest of the country occurred between 638 and 639, and we should expect the invaders to have begun, almost immediately, using the wealth of the land to build numerous and splendid places of worship — but apparently they didn't. Only two mosques in the whole of Egypt, both in Cairo, are said to date from before the eleventh century: the Amr ibn al-As, A.D. 641 and the Ahmad ibn Tulun, A.D. 878. However, the latter building has many features found only in mosques of the eleventh century, so its date of 878 is disputed. Thus, in Egypt, we have a single place of worship, the mosque of Amr ibn al-As, dating from the mid-seventh century, then nothing for another three-and-a-half centuries. Why, it has been asked, in an enormous country with up to perhaps five million inhabitants, did the Muslims wait over 300 years before building themselves places of worship?

The city of Baghdad, supposedly a metropolis of a million souls under the fabulous Abbasid Caliph Harun al-Rashid (763–809), has left virtually not a trace. The normal explanation is that since the Abbasid capital lies under

---

1 Ibid., pp. 72-3
2 Ibid., p. 73

the modern Baghdad, its treasures must remain hidden.[1] Yet Roman London, also beneath a modern metropolis, a tiny settlement compared to the legendary Abbasid capital, has revealed a wealth of archaeological finds.

No matter where we go, from Spain to northern Syria, there is virtually nothing between circa 650 and 950. Site after site throughout the Middle East has revealed an astonishing lack of archeology for these three centuries. Look for example at the stratigraphy of Byblos, an ancient settlement on the Lebanese coast excavated in the 1930s by a French team under Maurice Dunand. The excavators found rich strata for virtually every period of the city's history, with one exception: the three centuries between 636 (the Arab conquest) and the advent of the Crusaders (1098) produced *no material remains whatsoever.*[2]

Fig. 3. Stratigraphy of Byblos since Hellenistic Age

Stratigraphy of Byblos since Hellenistic Age

21st period	Ottomans	+1516 to +1918	**rich finds**
20th period	Mamelukes	+1291 to +1516	**rich finds**
19th period	Crusaders	+1098 to +1291	**rich finds**
	Crusaders of 110 build right on Byzantine foundations of 600		
18th period *enigmatic hiatus*	Umayyads + Abassids	+636 to +1098	<u>**no finds**</u>
17th period	Byzantines	+330 to +636	**rich finds**
16th period	Romans	-63 to +330	**rich finds**
15th period	Hellenism	-332 to -63	**rich finds**

---

1 In the words of Hodges and Whitehouse, "Abbasid Baghdad is buried beneath the modern city for, as Guy LeStrange remarked, so wise was the choice of site that it has served as the capital of Mesopotamia almost without interruption. Our knowledge of the city of al-Mansur, therefore, comes from written sources..." op cit., p. 128
2 M. Dunand, *Fouilles de Byblos I*, (Paul Geuthner, Paris, 1939); and N. Jidejian. *Byblos through the Ages*, (Beyrouth, 1971)

The same hiatus is encountered in site after site. In the Fars region of Nubia, for example, Polish excavators discovered Christian friezes and oil lamps dated to the "6th–7th century," but after that encountered an occupation gap of more than 300 years, when more or less the same types of friezes and lamps reappear in the 11th–12th century.[1]

If we look to the western extremities of the Islamic world, it is the same story. Spain, for example, is believed to have witnessed a flowering of Islamic culture and civilization in the two centuries after the Arab conquest of 711; and the city of Cordoba is said to have grown to a sophisticated metropolis of half a million people or more. Arab chroniclers appear to paint a picture of a flourishing and vastly opulent metropolis. Yet scholars now admit that "Little remains of the architecture of this period."[2] Little indeed! As a matter of fact, the only standing Muslim structure in the whole of Spain dating from before the eleventh century is the so-called Mosque of Cordoba; yet even this, strictly-speaking, is not an Islamic construction: It was originally the Visigothic Cathedral of Saint Vincent, which was converted, supposedly in the days of Abd' er-Rahman I (in the eighth century), to a mosque. Yet the Islamic features that exist could equally belong to the time of Abd' er-Rahman III (latter tenth century) whom we know did conversion work on the Cathedral, adding a minaret and a new façade.[3] Most of the Islamic features in the building actually come after Abd' er-Rahman III, and there is no secure way of dating anything in it to the eighth century.

According to Roger Collins' prestigious *Oxford Archaeological Guide*, Cordoba has revealed, in addition to the eighth century part of the great mosque: (a) The south-western portion of the city wall, which is presumed to date from the ninth century; and (b) A small bath-complex, of the 9th/10th century.[4] This is all that can be discovered from two centuries of the history of a city of supposedly half a million people. By way of contrast, consider the fact that Roman London, a city not one-tenth the size that eighth and ninth century Cordoba is said to have been, has yielded dozens of first-class archaeological sites. And even the three locations mentioned in the *Guide* are open to question. The city wall portion is only "presumably" of the ninth century, whilst, as noted above, the part of the mosque attributed to the eighth century may well have been constructed in the tenth.

1   Gunnar Heinsohn, "The Gaonic Period in the Land of Israel/Palestine," *Society for Interdisciplinary Studies; Chronology and Catastrophism Review*, No. 2 (2002)

2   H. St. L. B. Moss, *The Birth of the Middle Ages; 395-814* (Oxford University Press, 1935), p. 172

3   See e.g., Bertrand and Petrie, op cit., p. 54

4   Collins, Spain: An Oxford Archaeological Guide to Spain, p. 120

The poverty of visible Islamic remains from this period is normally explained by the proposition that the Christians destroyed the Muslim monuments after the city's re-conquest. But this solution is inherently suspect. Granted the Christians might have destroyed all the mosques — though even that seems unlikely — but they certainly would not have destroyed opulent palaces, baths, fortifications, etc. Yet none of these — none at least ascribed to the eighth, ninth or early tenth centuries — has survived. And even granting that such a universal and pointless destruction did take place, we have to assume that at least under the ground we would find an abundance of Arab foundations, as well as artifacts, tools, pottery etc. Indeed, in a city of half a million people, as Cordoba of the eight, ninth and early tenth centuries is said to have been, the archaeologist would expect to find a superabundance of such things. They should be popping out of the ground with almost every shovel-full of dirt; and yet almost nothing in the city can be confidently assigned to the eighth or ninth centuries.

Even when real archeology does appear at Cordoba, from the mid-tenth century onwards, the settlement is absolutely nothing like the conurbation described by the Arab writers. Indeed, at its most opulent, from the late tenth to the late eleventh centuries, the 'metropolis' had, it would seem, no more than about forty thousand inhabitants; and this settlement was built directly upon the Roman and Visigothic city, which had a comparable population. We know that Roman and Visigothic villas, palaces and baths were simply reoccupied by the Muslims, often with very little alteration to the original plan. And when they did build new edifices, the cut-stones, columns and decorative features were more often than not simply plundered from earlier Roman/Visigoth remains. A text of the medieval writer Aben Pascual tells us that there were, in his time, to be seen in Cordoba surviving buildings, "Greek and Roman.... Statues of silver and gilded bronze within them poured water into receptacles, whence it flowed into ponds and into marble basins excellently carved."[1]

So much for the "vast metropolis" of eighth to tenth century Cordoba. The rest of Spain, which has been investigated with equal vigor, can deliver little else. A couple of settlements here and a few fragments of pottery there, usually of doubtful date and often described as "presumably" ninth century or such like. Altogether, the *Oxford Guide* lists a total of no more than eleven sites and individual buildings in the whole country (three of which are those from Cordoba mentioned above). These are, in addition to the above three:

---

1 Cited from Bertrand and Petrie, op cit., p. 65

1. Balaguer: A fortress whose northern wall, with its square tower, "is almost entirely attributable" to the late-9th century. (p. 73)

2. Fontanarejo: An early Berber settlement, whose ceramic finds date it to "no later than the 9th century." (p. 129)

3. Guardamar: A ribat or fortress mosque, which was completed, according to an inscription, in 944. However, "Elements in its construction have led to its being dated to the 9th cent." (pp. 143-4)

4. Huesca: An Arab fortress which "has been dated to the period around 875." (p. 145)

5. Madrid: Fortress foundations dating to around 870. (p. 172)

6. Merida: A fortress attributed to Abd' er-Rahman II (822-852). (p. 194)

7. Monte Marinet: A Berber settlement with ceramics within "a possible chronological range" from the 7th to the early 9th century. (p. 202)

8. Olmos: An Arab fortress with ceramics "dated to the 9th cent." (pp. 216-7)

The above meager list contrasts sharply with the hundreds of sites and structures from the Visigothic epoch — a comparable time-span — mentioned in the same place. (It is impossible to be precise about the Visigothic period, since many sites, such as Reccopolis, contain literally hundreds of individual structures. If we were to enumerate the Visigoth structures by the same criteria as we did the Islamic remains above, then the Visigoth period would reveal not hundreds, but thousands of finds). And we stress again that most of the above Islamic finds suffer from a problem highlighted by Hodges and Whitehouse in other parts of Europe: an almost unconscious attempt to backdate material of the tenth century into the ninth and eighth in order to have *something* to assign to the latter epoch.[1] Consider for example at the fortress of Guardamar. Although an inscription dates the completion of the edifice to 944, we are told that "elements" in its construction have led to it being dated to the ninth century. What these elements are is not clear; yet we should note that such defended mosques, being essentially fortresses, must have been raised very quickly — certainly in no more than a decade. Why then are we told that this one took fifty or perhaps seventy-five years to complete? Bearing this in mind, we can say that there is scarcely a single undisputed archaeological site attributable to the first two centuries of Islamic rule; whilst there are, to date, hundreds of rich and undisputed sites linked

---

1 Hodges and Whitehouse, op cit., p. 84

to the Visigothic epoch. The first real Islamic archeology in Spain occurs during the time of Abd' er Rahman III, in the third or fourth decade of the tenth century (when the Guardamar fortress was completed); and it should be noted that the life and career of the latter character sounds suspiciously like that of his namesake and ancestor Abd' er Rahman I, who is supposed to have lived two centuries earlier, at the beginning of the Islamic epoch in Iberia.

What, it has been asked, does all this mean? How could the whole of Europe and the Middle East lose virtually its entire population for three centuries? And even worse: how could these regions then, in the mid-tenth century, be re-peopled by settlers whose material culture is strikingly similar to that of their seventh-century predecessors?

This is one of the great puzzles of modern archeology.

RETARDED ECHOES

As well as revealing an almost total lack of visible remains, the Early Middle Ages has presented other headaches for the historians. Characters and events of the seventh century seem to find strange echoes three hundred years later and to repeat themselves in the tenth century. Thus for example the seventh century in central Europe was ushered in by the destructive raids of the Avars, a nomad race of the steppes, into the German-speaking lands bordering the Alps and Bavaria. In the same way the tenth century was ushered in by the destructive raids of the Magyars, also a nomad race of the steppes, into the German-speaking lands bordering the Alps and Bavaria. Again, during the seventh century France was controlled by the Merovingian Franks, whose most important kings bore names like Clovis and Chlothar; whilst during the tenth century France was controlled by the Carolingian Franks, whose most important kings bore names that were strangely reminiscent of the Merovingians: Louis (Lovis) and Lothar, names clearly derived from Clovis and Chlothar.

In the same way, and very obviously, the Roman-style architecture of the tenth century, popularly known as Romanesque, bears striking resemblance to the Merovingian and Visigothic architecture of the seventh century.[1] This is all the more strange, given the fact that all building seems to have stopped entirely during the intervening three centuries.

Indeed art and material culture of every kind in the tenth and eleventh centuries seemed to mimic, in most incredible detail, the art and material

---

1 See e.g., V. I. Atroshenko and Judith Collins, *The Origins of the Romanesque*, op cit.

culture of the sixth and early seventh. Thus countless carvings and illustrations of royal and ecclesiastical scenes of the tenth and eleventh centuries seem to show kings and prelates in Roman-style churches and palaces.

And it was not just late Roman art and material culture which seemed to enjoy and incredible revival during the tenth and eleventh centuries. The phenomenon also included intellectual culture. It has been found for example that European monasteries of the late tenth century were in possession of huge collections of Greek and Roman literature, often profane literature, and great thinkers of the time debated the philosophy and thinking of the ancients. Thus Abbo of Fleury (latter tenth century), who served as abbot of the monastery of Fleury, demonstrates familiarity with Horace, Sallust, Terence, and Virgil. Desiderius, described as the greatest of the abbots of Monte Cassino after Benedict himself, and who became Pope Victor III in 1086, oversaw the transcription of Horace and Seneca, as well as Cicero's *De Natura Deorum* and Ovid's *Fasti*.[1] His friend Archbishop Alfano, who had also been a monk of Monte Cassino, possessed a deep knowledge of the ancient writers, frequently quoting from Apuleius, Aristotle, Cicero, Plato, Varro, and Virgil, and imitating Ovid and Horace in his verse.

Indeed the tenth and eleventh centuries present an altogether astonishing picture of intellectual ferment, especially coming immediately after three centuries during which Europe otherwise appears to have been reduced to a depopulated cultural and economic wasteland. Thus we find that Gerbert of Aurillac, at the turn of the tenth century, taught Aristotle and logic, and brought to his students an appreciation of Horace, Juvenal, Lucan, Persius, Terence, Statius, and Virgil. We hear of lectures delivered on the classical authors in places like Saint Albans and Paderborn. A school exercise composed by Saint Hildebert survives in which he had pieced together excerpts from Cicero, Horace, Juvenal, Persius, Seneca, Terence, and others. It has been suggested that Hildebert knew Horace almost be heart.[2]

If the monks were classical scholars, they were equally natural philosophers, engineers and agriculturalists. Certain monasteries might be known for their skill in particular branches of knowledge. So, for example, lectures in medicine were delivered by the monks of Saint Benignus at Dijon, whilst the monastery of Saint Gall had a school of painting and engraving, and lectures in Greek and Hebrew could be heard at certain German monasteries.[3]

---

1 Charles Montalembert, op cit., p. 146

2 John Henry Newman, in Charles Frederick Harrold, (ed.) *Essays and Sketches*, Vol. 3 (New York, 1948), pp. 316-7

3 Ibid., p. 319

Monks often supplemented their education by attending one or more of the monastic schools established throughout Europe. Abbo of Fleury, having mastered the disciplines taught in his own house, went to study philosophy and astronomy at Paris and Rheims. We hear similar stories about Archbishop Raban of Mainz, Saint Wolfgang, and Gerbert of Aurillac.[1]

The "revival" of Greco-Roman culture in the tenth and eleventh centuries extended to civic society and the law, and the laws promulgated by Justinian in the sixth century "had lain forgotten during the early Middle Ages, but in the eleventh century they were rediscovered and studied with vigor."[2]

On the one hand therefore historians find puzzling echoes of the seventh century in the great events and cultural developments of the tenth. On the other hand, events and processes which historians expected to occur only the in the tenth century somehow often began to occur precisely three centuries earlier, in the seventh as was the case discussed above, with castle building. The castle was, of course, the symbol par excellence of the Middle Ages. Europe is dotted to this day with the ruined or partly ruined remains of these majestic and imposing structures. These all, in the north of the continent at least, date from the eleventh century, at earliest. It is now known, though, that castle building actually commenced somewhat earlier than the earliest of the standing structures, and it is fairly clear that the first castles, usually of wood, were erected in the second half of the tenth century. The Normans, after their conquest of England, continued for a brief period to construct some castles in wood.

So, no one doubts that, in the north of Europe at least, castle building is a phenomenon which appeared first in the tenth century. Astonishingly enough, however, in the south of Europe, and in the Byzantine world, castle building appears almost precisely three hundred years earlier, in the first half of the seventh century.

The entire phenomenon of castle building in southern Europe, often known by the Italian term *encastellamento*, is one that has generated considerable debate in archaeological circles. In Italy, the process is associated with the abandonment of the scattered and undefended lowland farms and villages of the Roman epoch and the retreat to secure hilltop strongholds. These are recognized as the first medieval castles. In Italy, as well as on the Mediterranean coasts of France and Spain and in the Byzantine region to the east, these developments occurred in the first few decades of the seventh century,

1 Ibid., pp. 317-9
2 Painter, op cit., p. 136

and as such have been associated with the arrival on the Mediterranean of fleets of Muslim pirates and slave-traders. The activities of these latter are well documented in the historical literature of the period.

These early "castles," which appear throughout Italy and southern Europe from about the 630s onwards, are not the structures we now see standing in the same regions. Invariably, the castles or fortified settlements of the seventh century were replaced by proper large stone castles in the tenth and eleventh centuries, and it is these that the tourist is now shown. However, the tenth and eleventh century fortifications were built directly on top of those of the seventh century, and there is no sign of any structures dating from the three intermediate centuries.

We are faced therefore with the strange fact that castle building appears to begin in southern Europe in the seventh century, then ceases completely for three centuries, after which it again commences, in northern and southern Europe, in the tenth century. Even worse, the boundary between the area of seventh century and tenth century castle-building is often no more than twenty or thirty kilometers apart. Thus for example some of the castles of southern France which guard the Pyrenean passes, such as the one at Lourdes, were built in the tenth century, apparently to guard against Muslim incursions from Spain, whilst just a few kilometers away castles closer to the Mediterranean shore, such as the one at Montségur, were built in the seventh century to guard against seaborne Muslim raids.

Castle building was an integral part of the architecture and culture which we now call Romanesque, and the latter phenomenon has caused its own surfeit of confusion. Scholars are quite simply unable to decide whether Romanesque church-building, which indubitably flourished in the eleventh and twelfth centuries, commenced in the seventh or the tenth century. Both dates have staunch defenders. A striking feature of Romanesque architecture, the bell-tower, or campanile, seems to be assigned equally to the two epochs. Thus according to the *Encyclopaedia Britannica*, the appearance of the campanile is "variously dated from the 7th to the 10th century."[1]

We have seen that in the south of Europe castles were originally constructed to defend against Muslim piracy in the seventh century, though they appear in northern Europe only in the tenth century. If this were the only anomaly associated with the coming of Islam it would be bad enough; but the truth is that the arrival of Islam on the world scene poses a whole plethora of problems.

---

1 Encyclopaedia Britannica; Micropaedia, Vol. 2 (15th ed.) "Campanile."

It is widely accepted, for example, that Islam had a significant cultural impact upon Europe in the early Middle Ages, and indeed a whole genre of literature extolling the supposedly enlightening influence of Islam on medieval Europe exists. Yet the astonishing fact is that intellectually and culturally Islam seems to have made no impact upon Europe whatsoever until the second half of the tenth century — almost exactly three hundred years after it should perhaps have been expected. It is known for example a whole series of technologies and skills, such as paper-making, algebra, the zero in mathematics, etc., which the Muslim world apparently acquired in the seventh century, only reached Europe at the end of the tenth. What, we might ask, happened in the intervening three hundred years?

In fact, as the tenth century drew to a close Europe experienced a veritable flood of Arabic influence. We are told that Christian Europeans made their way into Muslim-controlled regions of Sicily and Spain, often in disguise, to avail themselves of the scientific and alchemical knowledge of the Saracens. No less a person than Gerbert of Aurillac, the genius of the tenth century, on whom the figure of Faust appears to have been based, had journeyed into the Muslim regions for this very purpose.

What began as a trickle in the late tenth century developed into a flood in the eleventh and twelfth centuries. The Persian philosopher Ibn Sina, of the late tenth and early eleventh centuries, became widely known in Europe and his name Latinized as Avicenna. In the second half of the twelfth century Avicenna's work was taken up by the Spanish Muslim Averroes (Ibn Rushd), who made his own commentaries and writings on the Greek philosopher. By that time European scholars were very much aware of Arab learning, and men like John of Salisbury even had agents in Spain procuring Arabic manuscripts, which were then translated into Latin. "Soon the commentaries of Averroes were so well known in Europe," says one historian, "that he was called 'the Commentator,' as Aristotle was called 'the Philosopher.'"[1]

The profound influence exerted by Islam upon the philosophical and theological thinking of Europeans was stressed by social anthropologist Robert Briffault, who noted how, "The exact parallelism between Muslim and Christian theological controversy is too close to be accounted for by the similarity of situation, and the coincidences are too fundamental and numerous to be accepted as no more than coincidence.... The same questions, the same issues which occupied the theological schools of Damascus, were after an interval of a century repeated in identical terms in those of Paris."[2]

---

1 Painter, op cit., p. 303
2 Briffault, op cit., p. 217

Again, "The whole logomacy [of Arab theological debate] passed bodily into Christendom. The catchwords, disputes, vexed questions, methods, systems, conceptions, heresies, apologetics and irenics, were transferred from the mosques to the Sorbonne."[1]

But this parallelism only appeared in the eleventh and twelfth centuries, over four hundred years after Islam took control of the Middle East, North Africa and Spain.

The ideological impression of Islam on Europe was not confined to the enlightened thinking of Avicenna and Averroes; there seems little doubt for example that the European idea of "holy war," as encapsulated in the concept of Crusading, was directly inspired by the Islamic doctrine of *jihad*. Islam we know was a military cult right from the start, with Muhammad himself apparently preaching the necessity of war and participating in over seventy raids and battles, often involving massacres. By contrast Christianity in its early centuries was an archetypal pacifist doctrine, and there are reliable accounts of Christian Roman soldiers being put to death for refusing to carry out acts of violence contrary to the teachings of their new faith. And Christianity seems (more or less) to have retained its pacifist character until the tenth and eleventh centuries. At this point, however, there was a dramatic change: from the mid-eleventh century onwards we find Christians involved in war against Islam in Spain and Sicily openly couching their struggle in religious terms — an idea that would have been anathema in earlier years, and no less a person than Bernard Lewis, the doyen of Middle Eastern studies at Princeton has conceded that the Christian concept of "Crusading" was in all likelihood derived from Islamic notions.[2] Certainly, the idea of war in the name of Christ was, in the words of Jonathan Riley-Smith, "without precedent" when it was first promoted in the eleventh century.[3] "So radical was the notion of devotional war," says Riley-Smith, that it is surprising that there seem to have been no protests from senior churchmen"[4]

The Crusades of course, to all intents and purposes, represent the Christian response to Islam's conquest of the Near East, North Africa and Spain. During the course of a few decades in the seventh century the Christian world lost half its territory and probably about three quarters of its popula-

---

1 Ibid. p. 219
2 In a speeach delivered to the American Enterprise Institute in March 7, 2007, Lewis said: "The Crusades were a late, limited and unsuccessful imiation of the jihad — an attempt to recover by holy war what had been lost by holy war."
3 Jonathan Riley-Smith, "The State of Mind of Crusaders to the East: 1095-1300," in Jonathan Riley-Smith (ed.) *Oxford History of the Crusades*, p. 79
4 Ibid., p. 78

tion to Islam. As the Christian response to these losses the Crusades make perfect sense; but by all logic it is a response we should have expected in the seventh or at latest the eighth century. Why then, we might ask, did it not materialize until 400 years later, in the eleventh century?

The aforementioned represents but a small sample of the evidence that could be brought to bear. Everywhere we look we find, from the late tenth and eleventh centuries onwards, a veritable flood of Islamic influence upon Europe — but almost nothing before that. Yet Islam appeared three centuries earlier, and, taking possession of the most populous and prosperous parts of the Byzantine realms in the 630s and 640s, we should expect its influence upon Europe to have been enormous from that point onwards; but nothing at all appears until the 950s or 960s. Why?

Mention of the late arrival in Europe of Islam's influence calls our attention to the fact, already briefly alluded to, that there are strange and striking parallels between the major events of Islamic history of the seventh and eighth centuries on the one hand and of the tenth and eleventh centuries on the other. Thus for example we saw above how Abd' er Rahman I, who supposedly founded the Islamic emirate in Spain in the mid-eighth century, sounds uncannily like his supposed descendant Abd' er Rahman III, who founded the Spanish caliphate and indubitably held power in Spain during the mid-tenth century. Strikingly, whilst Abd' er Rahman III's son was named Al-Hakam II and his grandson Hisham II, Abd' er Rahman I's son was Hisham I and his grandson Al-Hakam I. Again, the Christian *Reconquista* in Spain is supposed to have commenced around 720, with the victory of Don Pelayo at Covadonga; but the real *Reconquista* began three hundred years later with the victories of Sancho of Navarre around 1020.

At the other end of the Islamic world we note that the first Islamic conquest of northern India, by Mohammed bin Qasim, around 710, sounds very much like the next Islamic conquest of the region, around 1010, by Mahmud (Mohammed) of Ghazni.

And the three century "echo" is found also in Christian Europe. Consider the fact that the Scottish king Macbeth died at Dunsinnan castle in the mid-eleventh century. Archaeologists therefore expected to find remains of a typically medieval castle at the site — perhaps something resembling an early Norman fortress. What they found, however, to their astonishment, was a late Iron Age fort, which had apparently been abandoned in the mid-eighth century — almost exactly three hundred years earlier!

Macbeth was a known opponent of the Vikings, who were still raiding parts of Scotland in his time; and when we come to consider this people we are presented with a whole series of puzzles and conundrums.

It is known that the Viking raids were elicited by the Muslim demand for European slaves. The Vikings themselves were half pirates, half traders, who kidnapped large numbers of northern Europeans, from Russia in the east to the British Isles in the west, and sold them to the Caliphate, often directly and occasionally through intermediaries. As such, should we not have expected the Viking raids to have commenced in the seventh century, shortly after the arrival of the Arabs on the world stage? Why then do they only appear — according to accepted ideas — in the ninth century? Again, the Viking movement seems in part to have represented the final wave of the great Germanic Migrations, which had begun with the mass movement of various Germanic tribes into the Roman Empire during the fifth century. This was followed by further migrations during the sixth century, culminating in the arrival of the Langobards in Italy during the second half of the sixth century. After that there is nothing until the Viking wanderings, supposedly commencing near the start of the ninth century. Should this too not have been expected in the seventh century?

Quite contrary to accepted chronological notions there is much evidence, generally ignored in the textbooks, to suggest that the Vikings did indeed begin their migrations and expeditions in the seventh century. We have already seen how the first Viking settlements on Iceland display a material culture strikingly reminiscent of the seventh century Merovingians; and similar evidence has emerged from the other end of the Viking world. Over the past twenty years Russian archaeologists have investigated in great detail many of the earliest Scandinavian settlements in their territory, and have come to the conclusion that the earliest of these, as represented for example by the settlement at Staraja Ladoga, on the shores of Lake Ladoga, were founded in the seventh century.[1] From the point of view of textbook chronology and the accepted scheme of things this is an astonishing conclusion, though its significance has generally been downplayed in mainstream academic publications.

Apparently confirming the Russian finds, excavators throughout Scandinavia and elsewhere, as we have noted, have found seventh century Muslim coins in buried Viking hoards. This can only be explained by either of the

---

1 H. Clarke and B. Ambrosiani, op cit.

following: (a) The Viking Age began in the seventh century, not the ninth, or (b) The Muslims were using two and three hundred year old coins in their transactions with the Vikings.

Further evidence that there is something profoundly wrong with the whole scheme of things is found in coins from various parts of Europe which mimic Islamic coins of the eighth and ninth centuries. Thus for example a famous coin of the English king Offa (mid-eighth century) has on its reverse an Arabic legend together with an Arabic date. The problem here is that everyone agrees that Arab gold did not arrive in Europe and did not become the standard to imitate until the advent of the Viking slave trade, which supposedly commenced in the early ninth century. Why then was Offa imitating Arab coinage half a century (at absolute minimum) before there was any substantial economic contact with the Arab world?

At this point we must pause. From what we have seen in the present chapter it should be apparent that there is something profoundly wrong with our understanding of early medieval history. We find, between the early seventh and early tenth centuries a period of apparently total darkness. Classical civilization, which had survived both in the East and in the West until the 610s or 620s, disappears thereafter suddenly and completely. For the next three centuries archaeologists have been unable to chart any kind of development or activity. Even coins seem to disappear. Then, suddenly, around 920, towns and villages reappear. These are normally situated directly on top of those which were abandoned around 610, and the material culture of the new towns looks surprisingly similar to that of the older ones. The "Romanesque" art and architecture of the tenth century appears, just as its name would imply, extremely Roman, or more precisely late Roman. Indeed, Romanesque art shows a deep and detailed affinity with the late Roman art of the seventh century Merovingians and Visigoths, and so striking is the artistic and technical continuity that a whole generation of Revisionist historians has arisen who deny the very existence of a Dark Age, insisting that late classical civilization must have survived right through the eighth and ninth centuries and into the tenth. They can do this only by ignoring the archeology, which can find nothing between the early seventh and early tenth centuries.

As well as this archaeological conundrum we are presented with a plethora of puzzles of a more historiographic nature. Characters and events of the seventh century seem to find echoes in the tenth, often with identical names and circumstances. This is the case both in the Christian and Islamic worlds.

Again, we find that from the second half of the tenth century Europe experienced a major wave of Islamic influence — almost exactly three hundred years after Islam's first appearance!

What then, we might ask, can all this mean? Are these problems that can be solved, or are they simply impenetrable mysteries of the past?

CHAPTER 3: A MYTHICAL THREE CENTURIES

As the Dark Age mystery has deepened so it has called forth ever more radical solutions. Until recently the two most promising of these were: (a) That the Dark Age and the definitive end of Greco-Roman civilization in the seventh century was the direct result of the arrival on the world stage of Islam. Arab raiders and pirates, it was argued, impoverished Europe by blocking trade with the Middle East. Since the cities of Europe depended upon the Mediterranean trade for their prosperity, these now began to die; and (b) That some form of natural catastrophe or devastating climate change had decimated the populations of Europe and the Middle East, and this had led to the abandonment of virtually all important centers of population for three centuries. The chief exponents of these solutions were, respectively, Henri Pirenne and Claudio Vita-Finzi.

Notwithstanding the popularity of both these explanations, neither has proved entirely satisfactory and neither has consequently produced a paradigm shift. The main problem with Pirenne's thesis is the fact that the settlement gap appears in the Middle East just as much as in Europe. It may well be that the Arabs were destructive and that, as Pirenne argued, their piratical raids may have produced a "blockade" of the Mediterranean which cut Europe off from the prosperity and learning of the great centers of civilization in the Levant. Yet this should not have produced the almost complete depopulation that we find throughout Europe for three centuries; and it should most certainly not have produced a similar depopulation throughout the Middle East during the same centuries.

A similar problem affects the climate catastrophe thesis. What form of catastrophe, it has been asked, could entirely depopulate the whole of Europe as well as North Africa and much of western Asia for three centuries? And if any such event occurred, why did it fail to find a prominent place in the records and chronicles of the period? But an even worse problem is this: If a natural catastrophe of some sort had decimated human life in the seventh century, how is it that three hundred years later, in the tenth century, settlements and towns reappear directly on top of those of the seventh century, and these show every sign of normal and unbroken continuity with their seventh century predecessors. As we have seen, so striking are the correspondences between the arts and cultures of the seventh and tenth centuries that a whole generation of historians has emerged which denies the very existence of a Dark Age and insists that there must have been a normal progression from late Roman to early medieval in the tenth century.

These problems, so apparently intractable, finally in the 1990s elicited a solution so radical that it had never even been considered before. In 1991, German systems analyst and author Heribert Illig suggested that the years between roughly 615 and 915, or, more precisely, between 614 and 911, never actually existed, and that almost three phantom centuries were inserted into the calendar sometime in the Middle Ages. It was this chronological error, more than anything else, he said, which gave rise to the notion of the Dark Age.

The present writer has been aware of Illig's thesis now for over a decade, and researched it thoroughly before coming out in favor. I was initially attracted to the idea because it seemed to solve many of the riddles and enigmas surrounding the Dark Age. Having said that, acceptance of the thesis appeared (at first glance) to create almost as many problems as it solved. Copious records, in the forms of chronicles and annals, are known to exist from the Dark Age; and these documents cover the period between 600 and 900 in detail. In addition, they appear to be internally consistent. The Anglo-Saxon Chronicle, for example, and Bede, will mention the visit of an Anglo-Saxon king to France in a certain year, and the corresponding chronicles of medieval France will confirm the visit. Furthermore, if three hundred years were added to the calendar, how could this error have been transmitted to the Byzantine and Islamic worlds? Do not their records agree in detail with the western calendar? To argue that all these documents are false, we would apparently need to assume that they are in some sense fraudulent and there was thus a vast conspiracy that somehow took in all the nations of Europe and the Middle East. Such a proposition seemed utterly improbable.

Yet evidence appeared again and again which brought Illig's thesis forcefully to mind. The most crucial, for me, and the most decisive, came in the astonishing absence of Byzantine and Islamic archeology for this period. These regions, as noted above, were never overrun by barbarian tribes and should not, therefore, have experienced any kind of "Dark Age," and yet, in those very areas, from the three centuries between circa 615 and 915, we find precisely the same gap: an almost complete absence of architecture, plus a poverty of smaller artifacts and of original documentation. As with western Europe, the records and chronicles which cover these periods in the Byzantine and Islamic worlds were all written many centuries later.

The conclusion seemed inescapable to me: The "Dark Age," both in the east and the west, was a fiction; a phantom 300 years that have, somehow, slipped into the calendar. But how could such a thing have happened?

This latter question was, for me, the crux of the issue. It is scarcely possible that the Byzantines or Muslims would have co-operated with the western Christians in a deliberate falsification of history. Their histories, it is said, run in an unbroken sequence from the foundation of Constantinople and the life of Muhammad respectively. The Muslims even begin their calendar with a specific event in Muhammad's life. How could they have been mistaken about the date of their own founder's lifetime?

Before commenting on this, it is necessary to look at the whole issue of how chronology was calculated in antiquity and the Middle Ages. For the fact is, the calendars and dating-systems used in the Roman Empire and during the Early Middle Ages were very different to those imagined by the reading public at large and even by most academics.

ORIGIN OF THE *ANNO DOMINI* CALENDAR

The first reaction to Illig's thesis, especially on the part of those who have some knowledge of history, is to raise a series of objections, many of them of apparently insurmountable. How could such a falsification of history have occurred? Doesn't our calendar run continuously and without interruption from the first Christianization of the Roman Empire through to our own time? How could anyone then simply have added an extra three centuries to this? And why in any case would they have undertaken such a thing? What could have been the motive for such a distortion? Then there is the question of the Islamic world. Doesn't their Age of Hijra (A.H.) calendar match ours precisely, with major events and characters corresponding in terms of their place in European history? They begin their calendar with the life of their prophet Muhammad. Surely they would not have co-operated with the Christians in a deliberate extension of their history by three centuries!

All of these are valid objections, and need to be answered in a credible manner. The first of them, concerning the origins of the *Anno Domini* Calendar, is the most straightforward.

It is almost universally assumed that, following the conversion of the Roman Empire to Christianity in the years after Constantine, the peoples of the West immediately adopted the *anno domini* system. This, however, was not the case. When Constantine came to power the Romans employed a dizzying variety of calendars, some dating to the time of Alexander, some to the time of Julius Caesar, and others to the time of Augustus. Mostly, dates were numbered according to the regnal years of the reigning Emperor. In addition, a system named *ab urbe condita* was employed, which purported to date the years according to the number that had elapsed since the foundation of the city under Romulus. In reality, *ab urbe condita* was only devised in the first century A.D., mainly due to the efforts of the Roman chronicler Varro. With the conversion of the empire to Christianity in the time of Constantine's successors these calendars and dating-systems did not immediately disappear, and in fact continued to be used, in varying places, well into the fifth century.

With the formal abolition of the Western Empire in 476, the centralized Roman bureaucracy, with its records and record-keeping, disappeared. In its place there arose much smaller and localized bureaucracies working for the various Gothic, Vandal, and Frankish kings under whom they labored. These new kingdoms were all, in theory at least, Christian; and they still regarded themselves ultimately as subjects of Rome — though now Rome lay in Constantinople. The new kingdoms each adopted their own calendars and dating systems. These were generally, it is true, based upon the Bible; but they were not based on counting the years since the birth of Christ (*Anno Domini*), they were based instead upon counting the years since the creation of the world as outlined in the Old Testament. Christians of that period were not particularly interested in how long it had been since Christ's birth.[1] What they were interested in — what they were intensely interested in — was the

---

1 It is true that Dionysius Exiguus (c. 470–544) calculated, counting back through consular years, the number that had elapsed since the birth of Christ (525). However, Dionysius' computation was never used for official purposes and was almost entirely unknown in his own epoch.

question of how long it would be until Christ returned. The earliest Christians had believed that return to be imminent, owing to the fact that Christ had, in describing the times which would see the return of the Son of Man, said that "this generation" — presumably his generation — would not pass until these times arrived.

By the fourth and fifth centuries, Christians no longer saw the Second Coming as imminent, but remained very interested in the question of when it would occur (as they still are). In preparation for this great event, believers were not cremated, like the pagan Romans, but entombed in a vast and growing labyrinth of catacombs under the streets of Rome and the other cities of the empire. The bodily resurrection was something expected and anticipated. And it was this expectation that turned the attention of Christians to the Old Testament. In the Book of Revelation, John had said that, after his return, Christ would rule the earth for a thousand years — the millennium — and that after that time, the world would come to an end. Christians theorized endlessly on when this millennium would begin, connected as it was with the Second Coming of Christ. A clue appeared to be contained in the account of creation in the Book of Genesis. Here it stated that God made the world in six days, and that on the seventh He had rested. In one of Peter's epistles however (2 Peter 3:8), we find the statement that "with the Lord a day is like a thousand years and a thousand years are like a day." Christians began to speculate that the six days of creation might represent six thousand years of ordinary or profane history and that the seventh day, the Holy Day, the day on which God rested, might represent the Millennium, the thousand years during which Christ would reign triumphantly over the world. Gibbon puts it thus: "The ancient and popular doctrine of the Millennium was intimately connected with the second coming of Christ. As the works of the creation had been finished in six days, their duration in the present state, according to a tradition which was attributed to the prophet Elijah, was fixed to six thousand years. By the same analogy it was inferred that this long period of labour and contention, which was now almost elapsed, would be succeeded by a joyful Sabbath of a thousand years; and that Christ ... would reign upon earth till the time appointed for the last and general resurrection." (*Decline and Fall*, Chapter 15)

Thus, if it could be determined exactly how many years had passed since creation, it might be possible to predict when Christ's return might be expected. There arose then, in some quarters, an intense interest in the Old Testament and the Book of Genesis. Educated and sophisticated Romans, of course, trained in the thinking of Plato and Aristotle, could not look upon the

Book of Genesis as anything other than myth or at best allegory. Yet even at its height, the Roman Empire was not a literate society in the modern sense, and the great majority of Christian believers retained a simple and simplistic notion of the sacred scriptures and their interpretation. This would have been true also of the Germanic kings who now controlled the territory of the Western Empire. And even philosophers (and there remained plenty during the fifth and sixth centuries) could view the dates and figures provided in Genesis as, if not real history, at least providentially significant. The belief in science and reason does not automatically exclude the possibility of the supernatural.

Using the Book of Genesis then, and counting the generations of kings and patriarchs back to the time of Adam and Eve, it was possible to date the age of the world. Yet even such a simplistic and fundamentalist exegesis posed great problems, because the Book of Genesis was by no means clear as to when one generation ended and another began. The earlier patriarchs are said to have lived many centuries, and they had children throughout their lives. Using Genesis then as a guide to the Age of the World was thus a very unspecific "science," and it was possible to arrive at many alternative dates. Furthermore, quite different figures were supplied in different versions of the Scriptures. Thus for example the Septuagint, the version of the Old Testament published by the scholars of Alexandria in the third century BC, generally provided higher figures for the lives of the patriarchs and their offspring than later versions, such as the Vulgate. Jewish scholars around the time of Christ, utilizing manuscripts in accordance with the Septuagint translation, generally believed the world to be roughly between 5,000 and 5,300 years old. At a much later time in history Archbishop Ussher of Armagh, famously — using the Latin *Vulgate* Bible — dated the Creation to 4004 BC.

Scholars of the early Christian period, however, used the *Septuagint*. They were anxious to "speed-up" the date for the approach of the year 6000, and thus for Christ's return, and they tended to favor later dates. Thus one school, led by Bishop Eusebius and Saint Hieronymus, placed the birth of Christ just two years short of 5200; whilst another school, led by Saint Hippolytus, placed it in the year 5500. Other schools of thought favored 5300. All agreed, at least, that the year 6000 would see the Second Coming of Christ and the beginning of the thousand years of Christ's earthly reign.

Thus Christians of the fifth and sixth centuries were not particularly interested in the time which had elapsed since the birth of Christ, but in the time that had elapsed since the creation of the world. And when a Bible-based chronology was adopted, it was this Age of the Creation, or Age of the World, that was used. Nor would this system be abandoned until the eleventh and twelfth centuries. Only then did Christian Europe begin to count the years as *anno domini*.

The adoption of *anno domini* as a calendar reckoning-point has been traced in great detail by Heribert Illig, who has proved, beyond reasonable doubt, that it was under the Holy Roman Emperor Otto III that the system was devised. Illig has pointed to the well-known religious fanaticism of Otto III and had suggested that he may have wished to present himself as Christ's temporal representative at the time of his Second Coming. One of the New Testament prophecies about this event predicted it would occur when the Gospels had been preached to all nations. By the year 1000 (i.e., 700) this seemed to be coming to pass, as the Hungarians, the Scandinavians and the Russians all accepted the faith of Christ.

If Otto III's fanaticism produced the precise historical distortion we now have, there was another reason for the distortion, one that had much more to do with simple power politics.

WHY DISTORT HISTORY?

By the middle of the seventh century the whole of the Mediterranean had changed beyond recognition. Byzantium was crushed and close to collapse. Ever since the abolition of the Western Empire in 476, the Germanic kings of the occident, who now occupied the territories of the West, continued to give their allegiance to the Emperor in Constantinople. The gold coins they struck bore the image of the Emperor, and they accepted Roman titles bestowed upon them by Constantinople. When the office of Emperor of the West was abolished in 476, Odoacer sent the insignia of the office to Constantinople.

Henri Pirenne, who spent most of his professional career studying this period of history, was struck by Byzantium's all-pervasive influence in the so-called "barbarian" West. Germanic rulers may have had some degree of independence, but there were limits to what they could do. None dared offend Constantinople by reviving the office of Western Emperor. Although the Byzantines lacked the military resources necessary to establish real control of the western provinces (Justinian's attempt was only partly successful), their vast wealth gave them effective control. Whilst they could not send their own armies to punish recalcitrant princes, they could hire whatever military assistance they needed from other "barbarian" chiefs. So complete was Constantinople's control that only once before the seventh century did a

Germanic monarch issue coinage with his own image, rather than that of the Emperor. This was in the time of the Frankish king Theodebert I, who found himself at war with Justinian in Italy in 546–8. This singular display of independence on the part of a "barbarian" monarch was, noted Pirenne, bewailed by Procopius, who viewed it as a deplorable sign of decadence and decline. The next time a Germanic king showed such independence was in the 620s, during the reign of Chlothar (or Chlotar) II. Chlothar II was a contemporary of the Emperor Heraclius, in whose time, Pirenne noted, Byzantium first came into conflict with the Arabs. From the time of Chlothar II onwards, no western monarch would ever again mint coins bearing the image of the Byzantine Emperor.

The significance of this fact was stressed at length by Pirenne. Evidently the impact of the Persian and Arab assaults on the Eastern Empire during the first half of the seventh century was so great that the provinces of the West were able to detach themselves both politically and culturally. We know that within the few decades between the 620s and 640s, the empire lost much of Anatolia, all of Syria, and Egypt — by far the richest and most populous of her provinces. Constantinople herself was besieged by an Arab fleet between 674 and 678 and again in 718.

With the empire now weakened apparently beyond repair, the Germanic kings of the West, said Pirenne, began to assert their independence. This was signaled by the minting of coins bearing their own images; and it was to end in the formal re-establishment of the Western Empire under a Germanic king — Charles the Great (Charlemagne), king of the Franks. Thus for Pirenne the detachment of the West from the East, politically, culturally and religiously, was a direct consequence of the arrival on the world stage of Islam. "Without Mohammed," said Pirenne, "Charlemagne is inconceivable."

So far so good: There was, however, for Pirenne, one over-riding problem: Why did the Germanic rulers of the West wait a century and a half after the complete rout of Byzantium before re-establishing the Western Empire? Chlothar II, we remember, even before the death of Heraclius, had already shown the way, apparently around the 620s, by issuing coins emblazoned with his own image: Why wait another 180 years before taking the process to its logical conclusion and re-establishing the Western Empire?

From the point of view of Illig's thesis the re-establishment of the Western Empire does not represent a problem, but actually makes perfect sense, and in fact provides us with the real motive for the distortion of history perpetrated by the Ottonians. If we remember that the tenth century is actually the seventh, then we see that Otto I, who is commonly credited with another revival of the Western Empire in 962, after it had lapsed again following the death of Charlemagne, must actually have reigned in the seventh century, and his revival of the Western Empire would have occurred in 662 or, in Illig's chronology, 665 (Illig argues that 297 years were added but, as we shall see, there are very good grounds for believing the figure to be precisely 300 years). This of course is just a few decades after the death of Chlothar II and would mean that Otto I acted very quickly indeed following Byzantium's collapse in face of the Arab threat.

Under Illig's scheme then the re-establishment of the Western Empire occurs exactly where it should, in the middle of the seventh century. Yet the idea of a German Emperor was without precedent; and since no precedent existed, one had to be created. The precedent in question was to be an Emperor who has throughout the centuries held a semi-mythical status in European history: Charles the Great, Charlemagne.

Historians have long been aware of the fact that the Ottonians were the founders of what might be called the "cult of Charlemagne," though why this should be the case has never been adequately explained. The culmination of this process occurred early in the year 1000 when the Emperor Otto III visited Aachen. In the crypt of the cathedral he uncovered the relics of his ancestor Charles (or Carolus) the Great, who had died one hundred and eighty-six years earlier. Otto removed the burial objects and extracted a tooth from the skull. He also replaced the supposedly missing nose of the dead king with a gold sheet, before ceremoniously reburying him.

According to Illig, this Charlemagne was a fictitious character, and he notes the inability of archaeologists to find anything substantial of either himself or his supposed empire. Even his greatest monument, the chapel/cathedral at Aachen, is revealed upon closer inspection to have been built in the eleventh century — a fact proved in great detail by Illig.[1] Not even he could fully explain why the Ottonians would invent such a character and such an empire. Yet bearing in mind Pirenne's observations about the impact upon Byzantium and the Mediterranean world of the Arab conquests, the motive becomes very clear: As German princes claiming the title of Emperor, the Ottonians needed a precedent in order to legitimize their position. Since no precedent existed, one was created. Having then "created" a non-existent emperor and empire, this man and his scions needed time in which to reign; hence the creation of a couple of extra centuries in which to place them.

---

1 Illig, *Das erfundene Mittelalter*, pp. 187–305

In a pre-modern society this "creation" of two or three extra centuries was not so difficult to do: In those days there existed no public libraries or universal free education. Furthermore, with the closing of the Mediterranean by the Arabs and the termination of the papyrus supply to Europe after about 640 (or perhaps around 620 if Illig is right) there was an immediate and dramatic decline in literacy upon the continent. Almost overnight the Roman tradition of an educated and literate laity came to an end. Since all writing had now to be done upon the extremely expensive parchment literacy rapidly became the preserve of churchmen. Thus by the 650s or 660s we might imagine a Europe in which almost no one had books and very few could read or write. Bear in mind too that there was, as we saw, no agreed calendar or dating-system. In pre-modern societies in general people are not nearly so concerned about dates or times as are people in the modern world. To this day the peasant inhabitants of large swathes of Africa, Latin America and Asia often do not even know their own age, and we cannot doubt that an identical condition prevailed in medieval Europe. If a "date" or year number was needed, then the sum of years during which the reigning monarch had sat on the throne was generally the one used.

In such circumstances it would not have been difficult for the Ottonian propagandists to "enhance" the prestige of a half-forgotten or semi-legendary Merovingian king whose nickname (or perhaps alternative name) was "Carl" or "Carolus" ("the Warrior"), and who may or may not have briefly claimed the title of Emperor. Such a figure could then be used as the basis for an earlier Imperial (and German) dynasty. There are some grounds for believing Theodebert I assumed the imperial purple in 539–540, as he waged war against Justinian in Italy: Certainly he (and as we saw uniquely, before the seventh century) minted coins with his own image, rather than the Byzantine Emperor's. A fictitious dynasty, whether based upon Theodebert I or not, would need its own century or two in which to reign, and this had to be added to the calendar.

Again the critic might ask: How could the Ottonians get away with this? And again we must stress that what we moderns call "history", namely a body of literature outlining a more or less agreed picture of the past, along with an agreed chronology, did not then exist. In those days there were no public libraries, newspapers, and almost no education. Even today, after almost 150 years of compulsory education, and with extremely easy access to knowledge, how many people, taken at random in the street, could tell much about the life of Julius Caesar? Nine out of ten might say "a Roman Emperor," (which is in fact wrong), and have no idea when he lived. Perhaps one in twenty might give a few details of his life, including a guess as to when he lived. In a largely illiterate society, such as Ottonian Germany, no one would have known anything about the past. A few, a very few, educated persons, such as churchmen, may have been acquainted with the names of the great persons of history, such as Alexander, Caesar, etc. But of their lives and when they lived they could probably have said very little. The past therefore was an unknown territory, a foreign region which one might populate with the creations of one's own imagination.

Of course, we cannot invent centuries that never existed, if a firmly-established calendar, starting with a known event of history — such as the birth of Christ — is employed. If the *anno domini* calendar had been introduced when almost everyone believes it was introduced, during the time of Constantine, then the Ottonian kings certainly could not have gotten away with what they did. But the fact is, the *anno domini* system was not introduced until the time of Otto III, and did not become widespread in Europe until the twelfth century.

The motive then for the insertion of phantom centuries (and phantom characters such as Charlemagne) into history, was the revival of the Western Roman Empire. It should be obvious that a revival of the Roman Empire in the tenth century, after centuries during which Roman civilization and even the memory of Rome's existence became dimmed (as we are required to believe by the textbooks) is nonsense. But if Otto the Great was crowned by Pope John XII in 662, rather than 962, everything makes perfect sense. It was then that there was a crying need for a leader who could unite the depleted remnants of Christendom to withstand enemies who seemed on the verge of complete victory. Attacked on the north by Vikings, on the east by Hungarians, and above all on the south by Arabs, Christendom's days seemed numbered. Emperor and Pope, working together, hand in glove, might just save the day; might rally the peoples of a diminishing Christian Europe in one last effort. And the effort was not in vain. By the time of Otto III, the main thrust of the Magyar and Viking threat had been beaten off, and, towards the end of the tenth century (actually towards the end of the seventh), virtually all of Europe had accepted, or was on the verge of accepting, the Christian faith. Thus Harald Bluetooth had made Denmark a Christian country in 965 (in reality, if Illig is right, around 665, whilst shortly afterward King Steven of Hungary had indicated his willingness to be baptized and to bring his country with him into the Christian fold. This he actually did on Christmas Day 1000 or New Year's Day 1001 (or 700 in Illig's system) on which occasion he was reputedly crowned as a Christian king with a crown sent to him by Pope Silvester.

Poland too had accepted the faith, as had Russia (in its Orthodox form) a short time earlier. And here we arrive at a second motive for altering the calendar, the motive stressed by Heribert Illig. Since one of the prophecies of the Gospels was that Christ's return would coincide with the preaching of the Gospel to all nations, and since that prophecy seemed on the verge of fulfillment, Otto III, something of a religious fanatic, may, according to Illig, have conceived the notion that he should be the one to reign at the start of the Millennium; and that he, as Christ's temporal representative, should be the one to rule in his name. And so, working with the co-operation of the Pope, he decreed that New Year 's Day 701, the very day that the ruler of the mighty kingdom of Hungary was also crowned as a Christian monarch, should be celebrated as New Year's Day 1001. He could do this, we have seen, because of the general ignorance of history among the population, and by the confusion that reigned throughout Europe regarding calendars and dates. Some, as we saw, held that they were living in the Year 5700 of Creation, some that it was 5800 of Creation, and others various other dates. The point was: no one was sure, and confusion was the order of the day. Another element of chaos had been added by the arrival in Germany of Otto's own mother, the Byzantine princess Theophanou, who had wed Otto's father, Otto II. Theophanou came with a very large entourage of scholars and court officials. These brought with them their own Byzantine system of dating. Now, the calendars employed in the Eastern Empire were quite different to those used in the West. The Byzantines reckoned time, till quite a late date, according to a system designated the "Alexandrine Era". This actually counted the years, not since the death of Alexander the Great, but since the visit of the Emperor Augustus to Alexander's tomb (30 BC); an event popularly regarded as the official foundation-date of the Roman Empire.

However, other calendars, this time connected with the life and epoch of Alexander himself, were also known and employed in Byzantium. One of these was the Era of the Seleucids, which began in 312 BC. This counted time according to the establishment of the Seleucid kingdom upon the ruins of Alexander's empire, and was the one employed, for example, in the Hebrew Book of Maccabees, where it is known as the era of the Kingdom of the Greeks. Another and related Era was the Philippian, named after Philip Arrhidaeus, which began a few months prior to Alexander's death. Both these calendars were employed at Constantinople, and were connected, in the public mind, with the Age of Alexander. The Philippian Era in particular was closely linked to the death of Alexander (323 BC) and began almost 300 hundred years — actually 293 — ahead of the Alexandrine Era, which, remember, was established by the Emperor Augustus. This latter Era, we are told, was "the most widespread occurring Era," and was "long in use in the Orient."[1]

It will be immediately observed that one of these two similarly-named calendars dates almost from the birth of Christ (Christians were aware that Christ was born sometime in the reign of Augustus), whilst another, roughly three hundred years longer, dates from the death of Alexander. Since both calendars were actually used at Constantinople, it seems obvious that the scholars who accompanied Theophanou to Germany would have been well-acquainted with each. In the words of Illig, "We have therefore two eras which are very similarly named. One could indeed very well speak of two Alexandrian Eras. The difference between the Era after Alexander's Death and the Alexandrian Era amounts to 294 years."[2] Thus, in the latter years of the seventh century, which is — according to Illig — when Otto III and Theophanou really lived, by the calendar of the Alexandrine Era (counting from the time of Augustus and therefore also the time of Christ) it would also have been the latter years of the seventh century. But by the calendar of the Era after Alexander's death (the Seleucid and Philippian calendars), it would have been the latter years of the tenth century.

With such confusion, both in the East and in the West, it would have been the easiest thing in the world for the apocalyptically-minded Otto III to have declared himself reigning in the latter years of the tenth century, which would simultaneously have been declared the latter years of the sixth millennium.

This then, according to Illig, is how the 300-year error could have, or rather did, come about. We need not accept his every word to concede, I feel, that he has put forward a very plausible argument.

WHAT ABOUT THE DARK AGE CHRONICLES?

Accepting then that a German Emperor, in co-operation with the Pope, could have declared his own reign as marking the millennium, this still leaves us with a number of apparently very serious problems. (a) Hundreds or perhaps even thousands of medieval documents and chronicles, many of them claiming to have been written during the "dark centuries" (seventh to early tenth), describe the events of this period in great detail. Often the chronicles

---

1 "Ära", Brockhaus Enzyklopädie in zwanzig Bänden (Wiesbaden, 1966)
2 Illig, Wer hat and der Uhr gedreht? p. 179

and annals of one country provide detailed confirmation of those of another. Thus the Anglo-Saxon Chronicle, for example, will mention the visit of an English monarch to the Continent, and the visit will also be noted in the corresponding chronicles of Gaul, or whichever country he was said to have visited. How is this to be explained, without recourse to a vast conspiracy taking in the scribes — invariably monks — of all the nations of Western Europe? And (b), the chronicles and records of the Byzantine and Islamic worlds also agree — generally speaking — with the Western documents. We can scarcely believe that the Byzantines, and certainly not the Muslims, would have co-operated with the Latins of Western Europe in a deliberate falsification of history. How is this to be explained?

Let us deal first with point (a): There can be no doubt that the chronicles of Western Europe do provide a wealth of detail about events during the dark centuries; and the details provided in the various manuscripts are indeed internally consistent. According to Illig, all of these documents were composed in the eleventh, twelfth and thirteenth centuries, and none of them date from the periods they claim. Now, there is no question that the high Middle Ages was a period noted for document forgery. The best-known example of this was the so-called Donation of Constantine, previously believed to have been written in the eighth century but now widely recognized as originating at a later date. Purportedly issued by the Emperor Constantine, the *Donation* grants Pope Sylvester I and his successors, as inheritors of St. Peter, dominion over lands in Judea, Greece, Asia, Thrace, Africa, as well as the city of Rome, with Italy and the entire Western Roman Empire, while Constantine would retain imperial authority in the Eastern Roman Empire from his new imperial capital of Constantinople. The text claims that the *Donation* was Constantine's gift to Sylvester for instructing him in the Christian faith, baptizing him and miraculously curing him of leprosy.

Another famous, or rather infamous, example of this *genre* are the so-called Pseudo-Isidorean Decretals. These constitute the most extensive and influential set of forgeries in medieval Canon Law. Some collections of them included, for good measure, copies of the Donation of Constantine. These works, supposedly produced during the mid-ninth century but probably a good deal later, in north-eastern France, have been universally recognized as forgeries for well over a century. We should note that "Immense labor and erudition went into creating this work, and a wide range of genuine sources were employed."[1] Like the Donation of Constantine, the forgers' main object

---

1 http://en.wikipedia.org/wiki/Pseudo-Isidore

was to empower the Church, or more accurately, church officials; in this case bishops, who were thereby emancipated not only from the secular power but also from the influence of archbishops and synods. This was achieved partly by exalting papal power. The uses made of the forgeries form a historical study in themselves.

Document forgery then was something of an industry during the Middle Ages. These, as noted above, were not produced by amateurs but by men of immense erudition, who employed, to make matters worse, a wide range of genuine sources. All deceptions are more difficult to detect if they are mixed with truths.

Aside from those recognized forgeries, Illig and his colleague Nimitz have noted that a great many of the Early Medieval documents which are still regarded as genuine have an "anticipatory" nature. In other words, they framed laws which, at the supposed time of writing, were useless or redundant, but which later, during the twelfth, thirteenth and fourteenth centuries, became very useful indeed to the temporal and ecclesiastical authorities.

What then of the various chronicles and annals of the seventh, eighth and ninth centuries, which provide a detailed record of the kings, princes and churchmen of Western Europe in those centuries? These, according to Illig's thesis, had to be created in the years after Otto III, since, following his calendar reform, there existed on paper three centuries which never existed in fact and which had, therefore, no history. The three hundred years needed to be filled with something. Illig speaks of an enormous project, carried out in the eleventh and twelfth centuries, by the monks of various monasteries throughout the West, to provide a history for those three hundred years. He has drawn attention to the fact that modern textual criticism and forensic science has proven and is in the process of proving more and more of these "Dark Age" documents to be forgeries. It has long been known, for example, that at least 50% of the documents purporting to deal with the Merovingian kings are fake, and more recently this has been revised upward. Medievalists now talk of "a gigantic fraud more than 60 percent of all Merovingian royal documents ... forged!"[1] The entire guild of medieval historians, it is said, now stands "at an abyss of forgeries". The *scriptoria*, we are told, "bent facts 'like George Orwell's Ministry of Truth'"[2] A similar process is underway with re-

---

1   Matthias Schulz, "Schwindel im Skriptorium. Reliquienkult, erfundene Märtyrer, gefälschte Kaiserurkunden–phantasievolle Kleriker haben im Mittelalter ein gigantisches Betrugswerk in Szene gesetzt. Neuester Forschungsstand: Über 60 Prozent aller Königsdokumente aus der Merowingerzeit wurden von Mönchen getürkt," *Der Spiegel*, 29 (1998)
2   Ibid.

gard to the documents dealing with the Langobard or Lombard monarchy.[1] English history is far from being exempt: Illig has pointed to elements within the work of the Venerable Bede (such as his use of the term zero — i.e., *nullam* and the use of *anno domini* dating), which indicate that he actually lived and wrote in the eleventh century at the earliest, rather than the eighth.

Because the centuries between 614 and 911 never existed, neither, according to Illig, did the characters said to have lived in them. Thus most of the historical figures of this period, including some of the most famous, such as Charlemagne and Alfred the Great, are fictitious. Illig has now modified this somewhat extreme position, and has suggested that these persons probably did exist; only they didn't live when the chronicles said they did. A King Alfred of Wessex probably did fight the Danes, but he would have done so in the early or mid-seventh seventh century, not in the ninth. In the same way, it could be that the entire Carolingian Dynasty, of the seventh, eighth and ninth centuries, is little more than a replication or duplication of the Merovingian Dynasty (both dynasties were Frankish) of the fifth, sixth and seventh centuries. Kings in early times regularly had several names, and it would have been the easiest thing in the world to present a Merovingian king, such as Clovis I or Theodebert I, both of whom was without question a "Carl" or warrior, as an entirely separate character named Carl the Great. It should be noted in this regard that the life of Charlemagne displays striking parallels with that of Theodoric, the great king of the Ostrogoths, who controlled Italy and much of western Europe during the late fifth and early sixth centuries. Charlemagne also resembles in many ways the Merovingian king Theodebert I, who waged war against Justinian the Great in Italy during the sixth century and who may well briefly have claimed the title Emperor of the West. If Charlemagne is identical to Theodoric or Theodebert, this would explain why he is never credited with fighting the Muslims: Islam didn't exist in their time.

That the original Charlemagne did not live at the time the textbooks tell us is hinted in an obscure document named *Additamentum IV, Adnotationes Antiquiores, A.D. Cyclos Dionysianos*, which seems to have been an Appendix attached to the Easter Tables of Victorius of Aquitaine (A.D. 457). It was, in the opinion of Professor Laurence Dixon, to whom I am indebted for this reference, attached to the Easter Tables by a later (probably medieval) editor, not the author. Although the *Additamentum* is a wildly confused and indeed confusing document, it seems strange that it should place a Franco-German

---

1 Illig, *Wer hat an der Uhr gedreht?* pp. 228-235

emperor "Carlus" just after the reign of a Byzantine emperor named Anastasius. There were supposedly two rulers of Byzantium who bore this latter name. The first of these died in 518 and the second is said to have reigned between 713 and 715. Clearly then, from a conventional viewpoint, neither can have been a contemporary of Charlemagne; though it does seem strange that the first Anastasius should have died shortly before the beginning of the reign of Justinian (from 527), who was a contemporary of Theodebert I.[1]

As well as duplications, other characters and events, which were actually contemporaneous, were placed in sequence and the therefore made to "fill-in" a lot of time. This would not have been difficult to do, as the previous century (i.e., before 1000, or, in Illig's scheme, before 700) was rich in events, with continual military action against Muslims, Vikings and Magyars. Since there was so little accurate record-keeping (thanks to the severing of the papyrus-supply from Egypt), people's memory of these events, and their sequence, would have been hazy at best. In such circumstances, they could easily have been "drawn-out" and made to fill a couple of centuries. In this way the Viking raids, for example, would actually have commenced around the middle of the seventh century, say close to 640. Since they are well-known to have continued till just after 1050 (i.e., 750), this would have made the real epoch of the Vikings fall between roughly 640 and 750. Thus one hundred years of raiding would have been stretched out to make it look like two hundred and fifty years.

That real characters and events of the fifth to seventh centuries were in fact duplicated to "fill-out" the phantom centuries is argued at some length by H. E. Korth in his recently-published *Der Grösste Irrtum der Weltgeschichte* ("The Greatest Mistake in World History"), as well as in a series of articles on his website.[2] In one of these, "Doubles in the Early Middle Ages," he provides the list on the following page of alter-egos and probable duplications:.

I should emphasize that I do not necessarily subscribe to everything Korth has proposed in these charts, but he has, I feel, shown that many of the monarchs, prelates and great events of the Dark Age years appear to be duplicates and on occasion triplicates of monarchs, prelates and events of the fifth, sixth and seventh centuries.

---

1   Laurence Dixon, Letter, Society for Interdisciplinary Studies, Chronology and Catastrophism Workshop (2012), No. 1, pp. 4-5
2   Hans-Erdmann Korth, *Der Grösste Irrtum der Weltgeschichte* (Engelsdorfer Verlag, Leipzig, 2013)

FIG. 4. DOUBLES IN THE EARLY MIDDLE AGES

CHRONOLOGY YOUNG	CHRONOLOGY OLD	Dev.
700 C.E	400 A.D.	
Total solar eclipse. June 3 718	Gallian Chronicle. Solar eclipse 418	300
St. Aegidius (Abbot, but not martyr), d. 720	Aegidius, warrior (Name from saint?), d. 465	
Pope Leo III, elected 795	Symmachus ("confederate") elected 498	297
Inquisition against pope, 799	Inquisition against pope, 501	298
Pope Leo III rehabilitated, 800	Pope Symmachus rehabilitated, 502	298
800	500	
Charlemagne invades Rome, 800 (Dec. 24, 799)	Theodoric the Great invades Rome, 500	299
Charlemagne, d. 814	Carolus V. Nazon, d. 516	298
Judith of Bavaria (2nd wife of Ludwig the Pious), d. 843 in Tours	Chrodechild (2nd wife of Chlovis), d. 544 in Tours	299
Ludwig the German, d. 876	Sigibert I, d. 575	301
Total solar eclipse, May 5, 840	Beda Venerabilis: Solar eclipse 538	302
Franks subdue Hungarians, 862	Franks subdue Avars, 566	296
Total solar eclipse (south of France), Aug. 18, 863	Gregor of Tours: Eclipse, mid Aug. 563	300
Charles the Bald, d. 877	Carolus of Lander, d. 578	299
Ludwig II, the Stammerer (father of Charles III), 846	Carloman of Landen (father of Pippin), 547	299
Otto the Illustrious, d. 912	Carloman of Landen, d. 613	299
Arnulf of Carinthia, d. 899	Ariulf of Spoleto, d. 602	297
Charles III, the Simple. 879	Pippin the Elder. 580	299
Charles III ruling 912-923, d. 929	Chlothar II ruling 613-630	299
Heinrich ("majordomo"), father of Hadwig, d. 886, in Paris	Mummulus of Metz, majordomo, d. 588	298
Hungarian land seizure. Battle of Theiss, 895	Avar land seizure. Battle of Theiss, 598	297

Total solar eclipse (central France), 8 Aug. 891	Gregor of Tours. Eclipse 1 Aug. 590	301
900	600	
Eastern and western Francia united, 911	Eastern and western Francia united, 613	298
Ludwig the Infant, d. 911	Theudebert II, d. 612	299
Pope Lando Sabinian, d. 914	Pope Sabinian of Volterra, d. 606	
Victory against Hungarians, 911	Victory against Avars, 614	297
Arnulf the Bad, 907: d. 14 July 937	Arnulf the Saint of Metz, d. 18 July 640	297
Conquest of Mecca, 930	Conquest of Mecca, 630	300
Ludwig IV, D'Outremer. 936-954 (died Sept. 9)	Chlodwig II, 639-657 (died Sept 9-11)	297
Rudolf of Burgundy, d. 15 Jan. 936	Dagobert I, d. 19 Jan. 636/639	297-300
Cuthbert, burial 984 — Church for saint	Bishop Saint Cuthbert, d. 687	297
Leo VIII & Benedict V & John XIII: 936-972	Leo II & Benedict II & John V: 682-686	
John XIV & John XV: 983-996	John VI & John VII: 701-707	
1000	700	
Ethelred the Unready, d. 1016	Ethelred of Mercia, d. 716	300
Bede's tomb at Durham, 1030	Venerable Bede, d. 736	
Anglo-Saxon rule ends in 1066	"Continuatio Bedae" ends in 766	300

Korth also provides a series of tables outlining remarkable parallels between Frankish families of the early Merovingian period and Frankish families of the Carolingian epoch. These are listed by him under the title "Twins of the Pippin-Erae." Here are a few of them, complete with the various assumptions upon which Korth works:

ASSUMPTION I: PIPPIN IS PIPPIN I (PIPPIN OF LANDEN): DEV. = 80 YEARS

CHRONOLOGY Pippin I	CHRONOLOGY A.D.	Dev.
Pippin I the Elder, d. 639	Paeonnius (Pepin) 549	90-79
Theuderich II, d. 613	Theuderich I, d. 533	80

Murder of Theudebald and Theuderich of Metz, 612	Thedebald and Theuderich of Boulogne, d. 530	82
Chlodulf, Bishop of Metz, d. 696	Chlodulf (Theudebald) of Metz, d. 610	86
Queen Brunichilde, d. 613	Brunhilde (Nibelung), d. 531?	82
Chlothar II, d. 629	Chlothar I, d. 561	68-79
Sigibert III, d. 656	Sigibert I, d. 575	81
St. Mummulus, Bishop of Noyon, d. 665	Mummulus of Metz, d. 588	77
Brunolf III, Count of Ardennes, d. 642	Brunolf I, Count of Ardennes, 565	77
Hardwin of Saargau II, cited 670	Hardwin of Saargau I, cited 590	80
Walbert VI, d. 704	Walbert IV, d. 623 = Carllomen? d. 613	91-81
Hardwin of Saargau III, cited 699	Hardwin of Saargau I, cited 590	

ASSUMPTION II: PIPPIN IS GRANDSON OF PIPPIN I. DEV. = 75 YEARS

CHRONOLOGY Pippin II	CHRONOLOGY Pippin I	Dev.
Pippin II, d. 714	Pippin I, d. 639	75-86
Queen Plektrudis, d. 725	Queen Brunichilde, d. 613	88
Walbert VI, Count d'Ardennes, d. 704	Walbert III, d. 608	96
Walbert VII, Count d'Ardennes d. 725	Walbert VI, Count d'Ardennes, d. 623	98
Rekkeswinth (653-672) King of Visigoths	Rekkared I (586-601)	71
Wamba (672-680) King of Visigoths	Witerich (603-610)	70

ASSUMPTION III: PIPPIN III IS PIPPIN I. DEV. = 129 YEARS

CHRONOLOGY Pippin III	CHRONOLOGY Pippin I	Dev.
Pippin III d. 768	Pippin I, the Older, d. 639	129
Walbert VI, d. 704	Walbert II, d. 575	129

Walmar, Comte de Cambrai, d. 707	Wadon, Comte de Cambrai, d. 583	124
Alamannen-Herzog Gotfrid, d. 709	Alamannen-Herzog Gotfrid, d. 581	128
Alamannen-Herzog Lantfrid, d. 730	Alamannen-Herzog Lantfrid, d. 602	128
Alamannen-Herzog Theudebald, d. 746	Alamannen-Herzog Theudebald, d. 618	128
Baiern-Herzog Odilo, d. 749	Baiern-Herzog Odilo, d. 621	128
Tassilo III marries Liutpirc of Langobardia, 768	Tassilo marries Liutpirc, 640	128
Charles (after 27 yrs reign), d. 795	Charles (after 27 yrs reign), d. 667	128
Adalbald III, Comte d'Artois, d. 778	Adalbald, Comte d'Artois, d. 649	128
Arab invasions in Sicily: 827-830	Arab invasions in Sicily: 700-703	128

ASSUMPTION IV: PIPPIN III IS PIPPIN II. DEV. = 54 YEARS

CHRONOLOGY Pippin III	CHRONOLOGY Pippin II	Dev.
Pippin III, d. 768	Pippin II, d. 714	54
Unroch III Count of Friuli, d. 874	Unroch (Heinrich) Comte d'Artois, d. 816	58
St. Emmeram, d. 715	St. Emmeram, d. 652	63
Count Theodo (successor Odilo), d. 717	Count Theodo (successor Odilo), d. 654	63

ASSUMPTION V: PIPPIN I — C.E. (A.D.). DEV. = 220 YEARS

CHRONOLOGY CE	CHRONOLOGY Pippin I	Dev.
Ludwig of Italy, d. 875	Chlodwig III, d. 657	218
Justinus-church, Frankfort. Dendrochronologically dated 850	Justinus-church, archaeological date, about 635	215
Church of Torcello erected, 864	Church of Torcello erected, 639	225

Bishop Gunzo (Lorsch) since 856	Count Gunzo of Ueberlingen about 635	221
Lorsch, founder Rupert Cancor 856	Lorsch, founder Rupert Cancor 636	220
Luithari Graf of Alemannia, d. 880	Luithari, Graf of Alemannia, d. after 642	

ASSUMPTION VI: A.D. ◇ PIPPIN II AND PIPPIN II ◇ C.E. DEV. = 148 YEARS

CHRONOLOGY Pippin II (rsp. CE)	CHRONOLOGY AD (rsp Pippin II)	Dev
Tassilo III reigns since 748 as Dux	Tassilo invested as Dux in 593	145
Theodo I reigns 640-680	Theuderich I reigns 511-533	147
Richard Count of Ponthieu and Amiens, d. 810	Richard St. Abbot of Centule, d. 654	147
Alfonso III, d. 910	Alfonso I, d. 757	145
Synod at Frankfort 885	Concilium Germanicum (at Ffm)	154
Solar eclipse Nov. 30th 810	Solar eclipse report 664	146
Solar eclipse Spain Aug. 18th 863	Solar eclipse report Spain 718	145
Solar eclipse northern Italy May 5th 840	Solar eclipse report Switzerland 693	147

ASSUMPTION VII: PIPPIN IS PIPPIN III (FATHER OF CHARLEMAGNE). DEV. = 91 YEARS

CHRONOLOGY CE	CHRONOLOGY Pippin III	Dev.
Beranger King of Italy , d. 924	Beranger Count of Toulouse, d. 835	91
Adelchis of Benevent, d. 878	Arichis III of Benevent, d. 787	91
Wigbert becomes bishop of Verden 874	Widikund — Massac Verden 782 Bapt. 785	89
Hadrian II 876–	Hadrian I 772 -	95
Hadrian II christens Karl's son Pippin 872	Hadrian I christens Karl's son Pippin 789	91
Pope donates to Karl a 'Sakramentary' 872	Pope donates to Karl a 'Sakramentary' 784	91

Synod at Ffm, Karl condemns Tassilo 885	Synod at Ffm, Karl condemns Tassilo 794	91
Alfonso III, d. 910	Alfonso II, d. 824	86
Adalbert II Count of Maasgau, c. 819	Adalbert I Count of Maasgau, d. 737	82
Blaze destroys Dome at Worms 872	Blaze destroys Dome at Worms 791	81
Rupert/Poppo — Williswinda, d. 839	Rupert/Poppo — Williswinda, d. 760	79
Abd ar-Rahman II, d. 852	Abd ar-Rahman I, d. 788	76
Lorsch Porticus (Charlemagne) 795-800	Lorsch Porticus like 'Ecclesia Varia, 880	
Cologne Evangeliary — 956 — same style as Lorsch Ev.	Lorsch Evangeliary, after 865	
Solar eclipse Netherlands, Mar. 24th 852	Solar eclipse report Netherlands 760	92
Solar eclipse Italy, Aug. 18th 863	Solar eclipse report Italy 774	89

Summarizing the process by which a whole "Carolingian" epoch of three centuries' duration was devised, Korth explains:

> "Early in the year 1000 CE the Emperor Otto III visited Aachen. There he uncovered the relics of his ancestor Carolus, who had passed away 186 years before. Otto removed the burial objects and extracted a tooth from the skull. He replaced the missing nose of the dead [king] by a gold sheet, before he left the crypt."[1]

The body of Otto's noseless ancestor was mummified and sitting upright. Korth continues:

> A visit within the lost and rediscovered tomb facing the upright sitting mummy of Charlemagne... this may sound quite a bit overdone. But who could conceive the detail with the missing nose-tip? His "Charles" would have been inevitably disqualified as a ruler (let's just recall the fate of Justinian II, "*Rhinometos*")! There are just two explanations: The nose of the dead [man] was indeed missing — in this case, Otto III had found and opened the real grave of his forefather Carolus Nazon (480–516, "Charlie the Nose"). Alternatively, Otto [k] new about the missing nose, possibly from records in his family ...

> What was the intention behind this ghoulish spectacle? It did generate "evidence" for the newly set year-count scheme! Of course, a "Mighty Charlemagne" could not rule before the decline of the

---

1 H. E. Korth, "The enforced Millennium – no way to ignore Charlemagne," at www. jahr1000wen.de

Merowingians. But if Charles was real, all events and persons that were dated the old way referring to the incarnation of the Lord were thus shifted into past times long ago. In order to leave no room ... whatsoever [for] doubts about the validity of the year-count, the sheer existence of Charlemagne was pretended. In addition, to create ultimate credibility, events and doings of other rulers were assigned to "Charles":

Austrapius, the last Charl (king) of the Menapian people — gave his title and his name.

Carolus Nazon — provided the corpse (nose), year of death (A.D.), ancestry.

Chlovis I — did the conquest [sic] of the Francian empire.

Theoderic I — conquered Italy and moved into Rome [800 C.E.].

Chlothar I — subjected and christianized the Saxons.

Charles III. Simplex — used the KRLS — Signature and the coins assigned to "Charlemagne".

Otto I — obtained the ointment [was anointed] as emperor by the Pope at Rome.

One thing to maintain was the descendance [sic] of Charlemagne (and of Otto III) from the Menapian rulers that ... [would likewise explain] the ascent of the *Carolingian* dynasty. This could be provided without attracting attention by a fabricated (*Fredegar*) chronicle identifying *Pippin the Old* with *Pippin of Landen*, the descendant of the Menapians. The latter, so the chronicle, had installed *Chlothar II* on the throne. His descendants then served the Merovingian kings as *mayor domus* (chancellor) and, ultimately, they themselves became the rulers ...

No more action was required, in order to manipulate the chronology of the occidental world! The rest may be called "self-organization."

I repeat, whilst one does not have to subscribe to everything Korth says, he has shown very clearly that characters and events of the three "dark age" centuries appear to be duplicates of real characters and events of earlier years. As well as duplication and triplication there is no question that straightforward invention was also employed, also, as the Pseudo-Isidorean Decretals make clear, but these are not easy to identify — with the possible exception of certain obviously fabulous events said to have marked the lives of Charlemagne and the Byzantine Emperor Heraclius.

There remains problem (b). How is it that the Christian calendar apparently agrees with the Muslim calendar, which dates, or claims to date, from the flight of Muhammad (*hijra* or *hegira*) from Mecca to Medina? This is a problem of immense importance, and one that has a direct bearing on the whole question.

CHAPTER 4: THE PROBLEM OF ISLAMIC HISTORY

The Islamic world presents its own peculiar difficulties for the Illig scenario, as well as for conventional history. Here too, throughout the Middle East and North Africa, there exists an archaeological "Dark Age" between the mid-seventh and mid-tenth centuries, though in these regions such an epoch should not, under any circumstances, be expected to exist. On the contrary, it is precisely between the seventh and tenth centuries that Islam is traditionally believed to have experienced its apogee of power, wealth and learning. This period, far from being anything like Europe's Dark Age, is said to have been a Golden Age, an age during which the Arab world was the teacher and master of Europe.

But the researches of archaeologists have shown that this Golden Age left hardly a trace in the ground!

That is the problem Islam presents orthodoxy. However, it arguably presents Illig with a problem just as great: for we are told that the Islamic calendar, which counts its years from the *Hegira* (or *Hijra*) of Muhammad (his flight from Mecca to Medina, traditionally occurring in 622), agrees completely with the *Anno Domini* calendar of Europe with regard to the dates of major events and their sequence. If the Europeans under Otto III arbitrarily added three centuries to the length of history, as Illig claims, we can scarcely believe the Muslim would have co-operated in such a deception.

On the face of it, this seems to present a decisive argument against Illig; and of course it is one that his critics were quick to latch onto. For his part he countered by claiming that the Muslims did not use the Age of Hegira before the Christian use of Anno Domini, and he argued that the Muslims derived the idea of A.H. dates from the Christian A.D. system. He pointed out, for example, that the earliest Islamic coins which use the term "Age of Hegira" also give the Anno Domini date side by side. He also suggested that the early history of Islam and its expansion throughout the Middle East had been distorted for propaganda purposes, and that the real lifetime of Muhammad may have been centuries earlier than the sixth/seventh century in which it is normally placed. Thus for example he noted that, in terms of beliefs and practices, Islam is closely connected to the Ebionite or Nazarite cult, a sect of Christianity which was declared heretical at the Council of Nicea in 325, and which thereafter disappeared from the world stage, with its adherents apparently retreating into the Arabian interior.[1] Could it be, Illig has said, that Muhammad was a follower of these Ebionites, and that he actually lived sometime near the date of the Council of Nicea?[2] He noted too that the Council of Nicea occurred precisely 297 years before the traditional date of Muhammad's *hijra* from Mecca, in 622. In Illig's view of course 297 is the precise number of fictitious years added to the calendar by Otto III, and the fact that the same figure also appears between the Council of Nicea and the *hijra* seemed too much of a coincidence.

There is no doubt that the chronology of early Islam and the account of its expansion beyond the Arabian Peninsula is problematical in the extreme, and an increasing body of scholarly opinion has now come to the conclusion that the whole narrative of Islam's early history, including the life of Muhammad himself and the story of the early Islamic conquests, is at least partly — if not entirely — fictitious. This is a question we shall shortly examine in some detail; for the present, however, we note that even should we accept that early Islamic history as it is now understood is largely a work of the imagination, there remains for Illig an apparently fundamental difficulty: The fact is, there exist a great number of Islamic coins and inscriptions which predate the tenth century, and these artifacts are emblazoned with Islamic dates which seem to fully support conventional Muslim and (by implication) Christian chronology.

---

1 Shlomo Pines, *The Jewish Christians Of The Early Centuries Of Christianity According To A New Source.* Proceedings of the Israel Academy of Sciences and Humanities II, No. 13 (1966)

2 Illig, *Wer hat an der Uhr gedreht?* pp. 141-3

The earliest Islamic coins are recognized to be direct copies of Sassanid Persian originals. Typically these display on one side the portrait and the name of a late Sassanid emperor, either Chosroes (Khosrau) II or Yazdegerd III. On the reverse we see the image of a Zoroastrian fire temple. The only thing identifying these coins as Islamic is a short Arabic inscription, normally *bism Allah* ("In the name of God"), which is not written in the Arabic script, which apparently did not yet exist, but in the Syriac or late Aramaic script. Such coins also have a date, written in Pahlavi Persian, the earliest being 31, equivalent to 651 in the Christian calendar. This is recognized as the first Age of Hegira date to survive.

Numismatists agree that the first recognized Islamic ruler to imprint his name on any coins was Caliph Mu'awiya, whose mints begin with the year 41 (A.D. 661–662). Yet apart from the Arab name his coins still look typically Persian. We find again the bust of the Sassanid ruler, around which is written, in Persian, *Maawia amir i-wruishnikan* ("Mu'awiya, commander of the faithful"). The Sassanid fire temple still appears on the reverse.

It would also appear that from Mu'awiya's time the Arabs began to mint coins in Syria not based upon Persian designs. These are the first to mention the name Muhammad, though the general design of these artifacts is enormously problematical, as we shall see.

The name Muhammad occurs on coins of Persian (rather than Syrian) appearance during the reign of Caliph Abd al-Malik, who began to rule in year 66 (A.D. 685–686). In the latter's early mints the ruler's name is still written in Persian, whilst in the margin appear the words, in Syriac script, *bism Allah Muhammad rasul Allah* ("In the name of God, Muhammad is the messenger of God").

The last Muslim coins of Sassanid appearance are dated to year 89 (708), after which Caliph Al-Walid I issued a new type of currency upon which there were no pictorial images, both obverse and reverse sides being covered with Arabic writing. Still, dates continue to appear and these are generally in accord with the chronological sequence now given in the textbooks. Thus the Abbasid Caliphs, who seized power from the Ummayads in 750, continue to issue coins in the Age of Hegira sequence established by their predecessors. So precise is the Islamic dating-system, and so completely in accord with that traditionally provided for Europe, that we even find the English King Offa issuing a coin copied from an Abbasid original of Caliph Al-Mansur, giving the date, in Arabic, of 148 (A.D. 774).

Thus it would seem, if we are to go by the evidence of coinage, that there is precise agreement between the sequence of Christian European and Islamic history right through the time we call the Dark Ages.

That, at least, is the impression conveyed in all the textbooks. Yet there exist serious problems for conventional history with regard to Islamic coinage, and indeed with all early Islamic finds. With regard to coins, there are difficulties with the context in which they are found. Given the clear sequence described above we might expect seventh century coins to be found in seventh century buildings, with eighth century ones in eighth century remains, etc. But this is by no means normally the case. In fact, what archaeologists do find is coins of wildly differing dates found in the same strata and even in the same buildings or burials. This is the case, for example, at Samarra in Mesopotamia, where obviously Sassanid-looking Islamic coins of apparently the seventh century are found right next to others of the eighth, ninth and tenth centuries. The same situation is encountered right at the other end of the known world of the time. Seventh century Islamic coins, of typically Persian design, complete with Sassanid ruler's portrait and Zoroastrian fire temple, are found as far north as Scandinavia. It is known of course that the Vikings, whose trading relations with the Islamic world are well documented, imported large quantities of Islamic gold and silver coinage into Scandinavia; but this trade is normally believed to have commenced only in the ninth century (at earliest) and to have become really important only in the tenth. Archaeologists did not then expect to find Islamic coins of the seventh and eighth centuries in Viking hoards — yet that is precisely what they have found in a large number of sites.[1]

The discovery of seventh century Muslim coins in Viking contexts of the ninth and tenth centuries admits of only two possible explanations: Either (a) The Muslims of the ninth and tenth centuries were using currency up to three hundred years old in their regular transactions with the Viking, or (b), The Viking Age actually commenced in the seventh century.

The reader will, I think, agree that the latter proposition is by far the more likely to be true; yet to admit its possibility is to throw the whole of early medieval chronology into the melting pot, and that is something historians have not, as yet, been prepared to contemplate.

---

1   See Pirenne, op cit., pp. 239-40. Also, Ola Korpås, Per Wideström and Jonas Ström, loc cit.

THE ARCHEOLOGY OF MESOPOTAMIA AND IRAN

As stated, most of the Islamic world can provide very little archeology (if we discount the evidence of coins) for the early seventh to early tenth centuries. Nonetheless, whilst admitting that Spain, North Africa and the Middle East as far as Syria can show little in the way of material remains from the mid-seventh to mid-tenth centuries, historians do insist that there is one area of the Islamic world, namely Mesopotamia and Iran, which can supply abundant archeology for the questionable centuries. Traditional histories have of course always insisted that the very heart of the Ummayad and Abbasid Caliphates was located in Mesopotamia, a territory which is said to have boasted several enormous cities ornamented with dozens of royal residences, as well as hundreds of ornate mosques and public baths. The Abbasid Caliph Al-Mansur, we are told, established Baghdad, in central Mesopotamia, as the capital of the empire in 762, and the new city expanded rapidly under the legendary Caliph Harun al-Rashid (786–809), growing into an enormous metropolis with a population in excess of a million souls.

For all that, archaeologists admit that Baghdad of the eighth century has yielded few proofs of its fabulous wealth and size. The failure to locate anything substantial of Harun al-Rashid's city is put down to the fact that the eighth century settlement lies directly underneath the modern metropolis, and so has not been readily amenable to excavation or investigation. This for example was the explanation proffered by Richard Hodges and David Whitehouse. We hear that: "Abbasid Baghdad is buried beneath the modern city for, as Guy LeStrange remarked, so wise was the choice of site that it has served as the capital of Mesopotamia almost without interruption. Our knowledge of the city of al-Mansur, therefore, comes from written sources ..."[1]

Written sources say that the capital of the Caliphate was moved from Baghdad to a place called Samarra in 836 by Caliph Al-Mu'tasim, and the settlement established there grew rapidly in the years following. By the time the court moved back to Baghdad in 892, Samarra is said to have grown into an enormous metropolis of around one million people. And unlike Baghdad, the ninth century city of Samarra is still there, plain for everyone to see. The site was excavated by a German team under Ernst Herzfeld between 1911 and 1913 whose investigations brought to light an enormous urban environment replete with gardens, palaces, mosques and baths. Other cities of Mesopotamia and Iran, such as Siraf, have also been found to have flourished at this time, and to have left ample remains, or so we are told.

---

1 Hodges and Whitehouse, op cit., p. 128

At this point it is important to draw the reader's attention to a remarkable fact: All of the early Islamic centers of the seventh to tenth centuries which are said to have revealed substantial archeology are invariably to the east of the Euphrates River, in the former territories of the Sassanid Empire. Furthermore, whilst the advent of Islam in the former Byzantine territories — those regions to the west of the Euphrates — invariably reveals a destruction layer, the advent of Islam in Mesopotamia and Iran, the former lands of the Sassanids, reveals no such evidence of destruction; a fact which seems to suggest that the Islamicization of the Sassanid Empire was a far less violent affair than the Islamicization of the Byzantine lands. There is evidence of much greater cultural and economic continuity in the former than in the latter, with all the indicators pointing to a relatively peaceful transition from Zoroastrian to Islamic civilization.

Whether or not this be the case, it is clear that the eastern regions of the Caliphate, in Mesopotamia and Iran, enjoyed a great deal more wealth and continuity from the seventh to tenth centuries than did the territories of the west, the former lands of the Eastern Roman Empire.

Yet even in the east, the continuity which historians have laid so much emphasis upon is open to question. The dates provided by excavators at the Mesopotamian sites are often based on little more than a handful of barely legible coins. These, as well as the testimony of the medieval Arab chroniclers, form the basis of early Islamic chronology. But whilst the written sources speak of vast cities inhabited by millions of citizens during the three "dark" centuries, the spade of the archaeologist has revealed something quite different. Thus for example at Siraf, a Persian Gulf port of southern Iran, which is said to have flourished under the early Caliphs, excavators speak of five separate occupation layers between the seventh and tenth centuries, though the actual depth of these layers is little more than a few centimetres and would in no way be regarded as sufficient to account for three centuries of occupation. Richard Hodges and David Whitehouse point somewhat triumphantly (or with relief) to Siraf as one example of a settlement occupied continuously throughout the Dark Ages, though the only ruins they can actually show to the reader — a bazaar site, a residential quarter, and a house courtyard — all date from the tenth century.[1]

---

1 See David Whitehouse, *Siraf III. The Congregational Mosque* (London, British Institute of Persian Studies, 1980); also Whitehouse, "Siraf: a medieval port on the Persian coast," *World Archaeology* 2 (1970), and "Excavations at Siraf. First-Sixth Interim Reports," *Iran*, 6-12 (1968-74)

We encounter a similar situation at Samarra, though in an even more acute form. There we find that the traditional Arab account of the city's history, which Hodges and Whitehouse seem to trust implicitly, has been thoroughly debunked by archeology. According to the Arab histories, when Caliph Al-Mu'tasim established his new capital at Samarra in 836, the place was basically a wasteland, inhabited only by a few monks. These informed the Caliph of a former city in the area and of a legend that it would be rebuilt by "a great, victorious and powerful king." It was then that Al-Mu'tasim began construction of his new capital. That is the written story. Archeology, however, has shown that Samarra was already a large and important center under the Sassanids, whose king Chosroes I (late sixth century) extended the Nahrawan canal to the locality, thus opening it for settlement. To celebrate the completion of this project, a commemorative tower (modern Burj al-Qa'im) was built at the southern inlet south of Samarra, and a palace with a "paradise" or walled hunting park was constructed at the northern inlet (modern Nahr al-Rasasi) near to al-Daur. Later Sassanid rulers added to the settlement, and Herzfeld found evidence of a large and important Sassanid metropolis, replete with palaces, gardens, etc. The city continued to be inhabited and to expand under the first Islamic rulers. We know, for example, that another irrigation canal, the Qatul al-Jund, was excavated by the Abbasid Caliph Harun Al-Rashid, who began the construction of a new planned city, though this project was supposedly abandoned unfinished in 796.

Strangely, Hodges and Whitehouse make no mention of these Sassanid and early Islamic cities.

Thus Arab tradition proved unreliable with regard to Samarra's beginnings. It proved equally unreliable with regard to its end. Judging by the testimony of the historian Ya'qubi, archaeologists expected to find a city founded in 836 and inhabited for around fifty years before being abandoned at the end of the ninth century. This was not, however, the case. On the contrary, Herzfeld was forced to concede, on the evidence of pottery, coins, and other artifacts, the continued existence of the metropolis into the tenth and even eleventh centuries.[1]

Reflecting this, the *Encyclopaedia Iranica* admits to a "problem" regarding the traditional ceramic chronology at the site, conceding that Herzfeld's ex-

---

1 Herzfeld never published a detailed description of the site, only a series of aerial photographs. See Ernst Herzfeld, *Ausgrabungen von Samarra VI. Geschichte der Stadt Samarra* (Berlin, 1948). More detail is provided by K. A. C. Creswell, *Early Muslim Architecture* Vol. 2 (London, 1968), pp. 1-5, and J. M. Rogers, "Samarra: a study in medieval town planning," in A. Hourani and S. M. Stern (eds.), *The Islamic City* (Oxford, 1970).

cavations were carried out without due regard for stratigraphy, and that the city, contrary to traditional notions, continued to be occupied into the late tenth century and beyond:

> *The problem of traditional ceramic chronology.* At Sāmarrā the finds included lustered wall tiles from the palace of Jawsaq al-Ḵāqānī, al-Moʿtaṣem's residence. The ornament includes several familiar elements: half-palmettes, Sasanian wing motifs, and leaf scrolls. Some of the tiles are painted with birds encircled by wreaths. A second, larger group of luster-painted tiles, set into the frame of the *meḥrāb* (niche) at the Great Mosque of Qayrawān in Tunisia, has much in common with the finds from Sāmarrā.... Taking these two groups of tiles as his starting point, Ernst Kühnel proposed a hypothetical development of luster ceramics in Iraq: The earliest pieces were ornamented in polychrome; in about 246/860 a bichrome palette composed of brown and yellow came into use; and soon after the abandonment of Sāmarrā as capital monochrome luster was introduced. The tiles from the palace of Jawsaq al-Ḵāqānī were not found in place, however, and it is therefore not certain that they formed part of the original decoration. The reports about the Qayrawān tiles also leave room for doubt about the accepted dating (Hansman, pp. 145-46).

The conclusion that new wares were developed in the Islamic world in the 3rd/9th century as a result of the importation of ceramics from China was based partly on the assumption that Sāmarrā was occupied for only fifty years. Yet, although Sāmarrā ceased to be the capital in 279/892, silver coins continued to be minted there until 341/952-53 (Miles). Furthermore, according to Ebn Ḥawqal, who probably visited the area in ca. 358/969 (pp. 243-44, 247; tr. Kramers, pp. 236, 239) and Maqdesī (Moqaddasī, pp. 122-23), who wrote in about 375/985, parts of it were still inhabited. As the excavations of 1911-13 were conducted without regard for stratigraphy, all that can properly be said about an object from the site is that it may date from 221-375/836-985, but it may be even later. On the basis of the Sāmarrā finds alone there is thus no way of knowing whether new types were introduced all at once or at intervals over a period of a century and a half; for further information, it is necessary to turn to related finds from Susa, Sīrāf, and other sites.[1]

So, although Ya'qubi and other Arab sources claimed that Samarra had been occupied for only fifty years, in the ninth century, excavation has shown that it was in fact occupied during the tenth century, and that, furthermore, the artifacts found there can date from anywhere between the mid-ninth to the late tenth century, or "even later". This last comment in fact gives the game away. The fact is, the pottery and material culture of tenth/eleventh century Mesopotamia is virtually indistinguishable from that of the eighth

---

1 Ceramics xiii. The Early Islamic Period, 7th-11th Centuries, in *Encyclopaedia Iranica*, at www.iranica.com/articles/ceramics-xiii

and ninth centuries. The blue-glazed barbotine ware, for example, so characteristic of all the early Islamic sites of the region, is in fact equally characteristic of the tenth and eleventh centuries.[1]

Let's look at this again: Arab history tells us that Samarra, a vast royal metropolis, was constructed in the second half of the ninth century, inhabited for about fifty years, and abandoned around 900 or shortly before; and this is the narrative accepted by Hodges and Whitehouse, who present the metropolis as proof of a flowering Islamic civilization during an age of depopulation and barbarism in Europe. Yet what the archaeologists have found is a city constructed by the Sassanid Persians in the latter years of the sixth and early part of the seventh century, a city that continued to be occupied into the early Islamic period from the mid-seventh century and remained important into the tenth and eleventh centuries. So, instead of a fifty year old settlement, we have a four hundred year old one! Yet here again there is a problem. In a four hundred year old settlement we would expect strata many meters in depth. Comparable epochs in the ancient city of Babylon, for example, have produced anything from four to six meters. Yet the depth of strata at Samarra is nothing like this, and on the contrary would lead to the conclusion of a city settled only — as the Arab historians insisted — for about half a century!

What can all this mean? Here again we find that enigmatic hiatus that we have encountered again and again in the archeology of the "dark age" irrespective of where we have looked. Was Samarra then constructed by the Sassanid Persians in the late sixth and early seventh centuries and abandoned for three hundred years, before being reoccupied by the Muslims in the tenth century?

The only evidence for a ninth century Samarra (apart from the testimony of Ya'qubi), is the discovery of a rather small number of coins which appeared to concur with the latter. And indeed, Islamic coins are regularly held up as definitive independent proof of the accepted chronology. Yet the problems raised by these artifacts are enormous. Islamic coins of the mid-seventh century made their way to Scandinavia — a full two centuries before they were expected. And these coins are regularly found alongside others of supposedly the eighth, ninth and tenth centuries. The same phenomenon is encountered at Samarra, where coins of the sixth and seventh century (pre-Islamic) Sassanids are encountered in virtually the same strata as early Islamic coins of the latter seventh, eighth, ninth and tenth centuries.

---

1 Ibid.

Something more shall be said about this thoroughly confusing topic at a later stage; suffice here to note that there are very good grounds for believing the numbers found on these (supposedly seventh, eighth, ninth and tenth century) coins do *not* represent Age of Hegira dates, and that, furthermore, the entire system of notation was changed on more than one occasion by the early Muslim rulers.

Whatever we might say about traditional written histories and the dating of coins, we can say that the archeology of Samarra and the other flourishing urban centers of Mesopotamia/Iran of the early Caliphate, looks as if it could equally belong, on the one hand, in the late Sassanid epoch, and, on the other, to the tenth or eleventh centuries. Furthermore, the depth of strata and the amount of archeology uncovered would suffice for about a century at maximum, but certainly not the four centuries which apparently separate the rise of Islam from the abandonment of Samarra and Siraf in the eleventh century.

THE CHRONOLOGY OF ISLAM'S EARLY EXPANSION

We have seen that in Illig's scheme Islam would have reached the western Mediterranean and Spain several decades before the textbooks tell us. Thus if Abd' er Rahman III, who left abundant archeology in Spain from the mid-tenth century onwards, is the same person as Abd' er Rahman I, who supposedly founded the Spanish emirate two hundred years earlier (but who left little or no trace in the archaeological record), then both characters must in fact be moved to the mid-seventh century. Illig's tenth century, after all, in all particulars, is identical to the seventh.

And there is much other evidence pointing in the same direction; pointing in fact to an Islamic expansion across the Middle East at least two to three decades earlier than is commonly supposed.

The real break-off point between classical civilization and the medieval world is 614, the year of the fall of Syria/Palestine and Jerusalem to the Persian forces of Chosroes II. It was then, or in the decade immediately after, that the great cities of Asia Minor and Syria were destroyed or abandoned, never to rise again. That there was no attempt to repair them after the end of the Persian War (627) indicates that there was insufficient time to do so before the coming of the Arabs (supposedly in 638). Yet in a decade we might expect some signs of revival or rebuilding. That there were almost none could suggest that the arrival of the Arabs and Islam on the world stage was closer to the time of the Persian War than is allowed.

It is traditionally believed that Muslim armies did not emerge from Arabia until after Muhammad's death in 638. Yet there is evidence to suggest otherwise. A letter exists purportedly from Muhammad to Chosroes II, inviting him to embrace Islam. Whether this communication is genuine or not (actually, it is without question a forgery), it does illustrate an important truth: The Persians had a long history of religious antagonism towards Christianity and towards Byzantium, and as such would have been natural allies of the Arabs against the Romans. During the latter years of the sixth century Chosroes II's grandfather Chosroes I had gone to the assistance of the southern Arabs whose country Yemen had been annexed by the Christian Abyssinians. During this period the Sassanids were extremely active in building alliances throughout the Arabian Peninsula, and it is known that large contingents of Arab warriors served in the Persian armies. And the war between Chosroes II and Heraclius which erupted in 602 had from the very beginning all the characteristics of a religious conflict — a veritable *jihad*, no less. The Persians, along with numerous Arab allies, took Jerusalem in 614 and carried out a general massacre of the Christian population,[1] after which they looted the churches and seized some of Christendom's most sacred relics — including the Holy Cross upon which Christ was crucified. The story told by the Byzantines of how Heraclius, against all the odds, turned the tide of war and won back the sacred relics, strikes one as fictitious. Persian sources make no mention of Chosroes' supposed defeat at the hands of the Byzantines. On the contrary, he is known in Iranian tradition as *Apervez,* (later abbreviated to *Pervez*) "the undefeatable" or "ever-victorious." The most important Iranian source, the *Shahnameh* merely records how Chosroes was killed by his son Shirouyeh, who desired his father's beautiful wife Shirin.

It would appear then that the Byzantines may have been falsifying history with regard to Heraclius' later career, and it is just with the latter's reign that the dim and little-known period we now call the Dark Ages commences. An earlier war between Romans and Persians, in the time of Alexander Severus (third century), was equally doctored by Roman chroniclers to make its outcome more palatable, as Gibbon dryly remarks: "If we credit what should seem the most authentic of all records, an oration, still extant, delivered by the emperor himself to the senate, we must allow that the victory of Alexander Severus was not inferior to any of those formerly obtained over the Persians by the son of Philip [Alexander the Great]." However, "far from being inclined to believe that the arms of Alexander [Severus] obtained

---

1 See Gibbon, *Decline and Fall*, Chapter 46

any memorable advantage over the Persians, we are induced to suspect that all this blaze of imaginary glory was designed to conceal some real disgrace."[1]

A possible motive — aside from the need to disguise a humiliating defeat — for the Byzantine's rewriting of Heraclius' life and career, is examined in the next chapter.

Illig has suggested that the Persians encountered Islam in Syria and, seeing the latter as a valuable ally against Byzantium, joined forces with the Arabs. It is not inconceivable that senior members of the Persian ruling class may have converted to Islam and gradually imposed the new faith upon the populace. This would explain why the Arabs were able to "conquer" — with such apparent ease — the mighty and invincible Persian Empire, an empire that had withstood the best efforts of Rome to subdue it for seven centuries.[2] And it would further explain why early Islam is so thoroughly Persian in character. The Islamic symbol *par excellence*, for example, the crescent moon enclosing a star, is Persian: the motif is encountered repeatedly on monumental Iranian art and Sassanid coins.

The Persian influence is indeed all pervasive. The great Islamic cities of the time, including Baghdad and Samarra, followed a typically Persian ground-plan, with Persian features such as "paradises" or ornamental gardens. The artwork found at Samarra, including pottery, painting, and architectural features, is all thoroughly Persian. It is well known too that the early caliphs ruled largely, if not completely, through a Persian bureaucracy.[3] And we remind ourselves that the earliest Islamic coins are straightforwardly Persian, usually with the addition of an Arab, or rather Syriac, phrase such as *besm Allah*, and with the name of Chosroes II or his successor Yazdegerd III. But in all other particulars they are indistinguishable from Sassanid currency. According to the *Encyclopdaedia Iranica*:

> These coins usually have a portrait of a Sasanian emperor with an honorific inscription and various ornaments. To the right of the portrait is a ruler's or governor's name written in Pahlavi script. On the reverse there is a Zoroastrian fire altar with attendants on either side. At the far left is the year of issue expressed in words, and at the

---

1   Ibid., Chapter 8

2   It should be noted that the accepted narrative of Islam's early expansion beyond Arabia just does not make sense. That the Arabs, a numerically tiny and backward people, should simultaneously attack and overcome both the might of Byzantium and of Sassanid Persia is quite simply beyond belief. And it is no use to plead that these powers were "exhausted" by the war they had just recently waged against each other. Victorious armies do not tend to be "exhausted", irrespective of their losses. Witness the mighty Soviet army at the end of World War II, compared to the weak and incompetent Soviet army at the beginning of the same conflict. Thus Heraclius' Byzantine army, newly victorious over the Persians, would have been no pushover.

3   See Trevor-Roper, op cit., p. 142

right is the place of minting. In all these features, the Arab-Sasanian coinages are similar to Sasanian silver drahms. The major difference between the two series is the presence of some additional Arabic inscription on most coins issued under Muslim authority, but some coins with no Arabic can still be attributed to the Islamic period. The Arab-Sasanian coinages are not imitations, since they were surely designed and manufactured by the same people as the late Sasanian issues, illustrating the continuity of administration and economic life in the early years of Muslim rule in Iran.[1]

Note the remark: "The Arab-Sasanian coinages are not imitations," but were "designed and manufactured by the same people as the late Sasanian issues." We note also that the date provided on these artifacts is written in Persian script, and it would appear that those who minted the coins, native Persians, did not understand Arabic. We hear that under the Arabs the mints were "evidently allowed to go on as before," and that there are "a small number of coins indistinguishable from the drahms of the last emperor, Yazdegerd III, dated during his reign but after the Arab capture of the cities of issue. It was only when Yazdegerd died (A.D. 651) that some mark of Arab authority was added to the coinage."[2] Even more puzzling is the fact that the most common coins during the first decades of Islamic rule were those of Chosroes II, and many of these too bear the Arabic inscription (written, as mentioned above, in the Syriac script) *besm Allah*. Now, it is just conceivable that invading Arabs might have issued slightly amended coins of the last Sassanid monarch, Yazdegerd III, but why continue to issue money in the name of a previous Sassanid king (Chosroes II), one who, supposedly, had died ten years earlier? This surely stretches credulity.

Fig. 5 A. Early Islamic coin of Persian design showing Sassanid Emperor Yazdegerd III and Zoroastrian fire temple on reverse.

1 "Arab-Sasanian Coins," *Encyclopdaedia Iranica*, at www.iranica.com/articles/arab-sasanian-coins
2 Ibid.

Fig.5 B. Islamic coin of Caliph Mu'awiya showing figure holding a cross.

Did then Chosroes II convert to Islam as part of Persia's ongoing Holy War against Christian Byzantium? Conventional history tells us that Chosroes' successor Yazdegerd III was the last of the pre-Islamic rulers of Iran, and that, in his time Caliph Umar conquered the country. Yet the Persian poet Firdowsi, who seems to have possessed a detailed knowledge of the period, mentions no Arab conquest at all. The Arabs are mentioned, but not as enemies of Yazdegerd III. The latter, who is portrayed as a villain, is killed by a miller, not by the Arabs (who are also portrayed as villains). Indeed, the events described by Firdowsi have all the hallmarks of a Persian civil war. Is it possible that during the time of Yazdegerd III an internecine war erupted between an "Arabizing" group and a more traditional Persian faction? Later Islamic propagandists could have portrayed this conflict as an Arab "conquest" of Persia.

The evidence of archeology, as we shall see, fully supports the above hypothesis.

OTHER QUESTION MARKS ABOUT EARLY ISLAM

If the questions raised about Islam's early expansion outlined above seem dramatic, then the even greater questions which have recently emerged regarding the origins of Islam and even the life of Muhammad will seem sensational. Generated by the current topicality of Islam, the past few years have seen a proliferation of studies into the faith's roots; studies which have begun to subject it to the same critical examination that Christianity has undergone now for a century and a half. And the results of these studies have revealed that almost everything traditionally accepted about Islam's origins cannot stand up to criticism. It has been shown, for example, that the Qur'an could not possibly have been written when tradition says it was and that the very existence of a man called Muhammad is called into question.

The numerous titles which have appeared recently include in particular *The Syro-Aramaic Reading of the Koran: A Contribution to the Decoding of the Language of the Koran* by Christoph Luxenberg (2007) and *The Hidden Origins of Islam: New Research into its Early History*, a series of essays edited by Karl-Heinz Ohlig and Gerd-R Puin (2009).

Upon the publication of Luxenberg's book, the popular media (perhaps typically) focused on his claim that the 72 virgins promised to Islamic martyrs was a mistranslation, and that what was actually on offer was 72 raisins, or grapes. Yet this was the very least of what Luxenberg was saying, the full import of which was ignored in the newspapers. In fact, he was claiming that the original language of the Qur'an was not Arabic (where the questionable word is read as "virgins") but Syriac or Aramaic, where the same word would translate as "grapes." He was furthermore claiming, sensationally enough, that the Qur'an was originally a Syriac Christian devotional text and had nothing to do with Muhammad or Islam.

Taking the lead from Luxenberg, several more recent studies have denied the existence of anyone called Muhammad in the first place. Amongst the better known of these are Norbert Pressburg's *Good Bye Mohammed* (2009) and Robert Spencer's *Did Muhammad Exist? An Enquiry into Islam's Obscure Origins* (2012). Though both Spencer and Pressburg are seen as critics of Islam, their books examine the evidence, both archaeological and textual, in a scholarly fashion, and the conclusions they reach are devastating to the accepted narrative of Islam's origins and early history.

Some of the earliest recognizably Muslim artifacts, as we saw above, are coins, and the Spencer and Pressburg books consider the evidence of these in detail. There we find that not all early Islamic mints were based on Persian prototypes. Some, from Syria, look more Byzantine in appearance. The first of these, astonishingly enough, show a figure holding a cross. Some of these coins, the earliest of which are from the time of Caliph Mu'awiya and traditionally dated between 661 and 672, have the name "Muhammad" beside the figure with the cross. Not surprisingly, these artifacts do not figure prominently in popularized accounts of the development of Islamic coinage; they are far too problematic. To begin with, they violate a number of principles which are now regarded as fundamental to the Islamic faith. They display an image — perhaps even that of the prophet Muhammad; and even worse, they have that image holding a cross. Among Muslims the cross is anathema; it is an anti-sign. Islamic tradition denies that Jesus (whom it admits was a prophet) died on the cross and dissociates Jesus entirely from what it considers a symbol of shame.

Evidently when these coins were minted, in the middle of the seventh century, the Islamic theology with which we are now familiar had not evolved. But there is even worse. It would appear that the figure holding the cross, beside which sometimes appears the name "Muhammad," may not represent the prophet of Islam at all, but Jesus. As Spencer emphasizes, the word "Muhammad" in Arabic and Syriac implies the "praised one" or "chosen one," and may be a title or epithet as much as a real name. As a personal name Muhammad is in fact unattested before the seventh century, and indeed, considering the word's meaning it is unlikely that anyone named Muhammad ever existed in Arabia before this time. Parents do not normally call their child by titles such as "chosen one." In short, even if an Arab prophet and war-leader called Muhammad existed, it is highly likely that this name was only given to him after his death, or at least late in life. But the fact that the figure on the coins is holding a cross would indicate very strongly that the "praised one" in question was not the prophet of Islam, but Jesus of Nazareth. And this is made all the more likely when we consider the strong links between Jesus and Muhammad in Islamic tradition. According to this, Jesus foretold the coming of Muhammad, who he named Ahmed. The "Muhammad prophecy" of Jesus is referred to by Ibn Ishaq, Muhammad's earliest biographer (mid-eighth century), who remarked that in the Gospel passage where Jesus refers to the coming of the Comforter [Aramaic *Munahhemana*], he is actually referring to the coming of Muhammad. Ibn Ishaq explains: "the *Munahhemana* (God bless and preserve him!) in Syriac is Muhammad; in Greek he is paraclete." However, Ibn Ishaq's English translator Alfred Guillaume notes that the word *Munahhemana* "in the Eastern patristic literature ... is applied to Our Lord Himself". The original bearer of the title "praised one," said Guillaume, was Jesus, and this title and the accompanying prophecy were "skillfully manipulated to provide the reading we have" in Ibn Ishaq's biography.[1]

What can all this possibly mean? Is it possible that the "prophet Muhammad" was invented several decades after Islam, or the faith we now call Islam, appeared on the world stage? This is a possibility considered by Spencer and he provides very good grounds for doing so.

As Spencer notes, none of the early texts or inscriptions of the seventh century which refer to the Muslims mention either Muhammad, the Qur'an or even the word Islam. Indeed, inscriptions — both on coins and elsewhere

---

1 Alfred Guillaume, "The Version of the Gospels Used in Medina Circa 700 AD." *Al-Andalus* 15 (1950), pp. 289-96

— of the early Islamic authorities use terms and expressions not found in the Qur'an. This, among other things, has prompted several historians to suggest that the Qur'an did not then exist and would not exist until near the end of the seventh century — or even the early eighth century.

The evidence, taken together, would suggest that the "Islam" which conquered the Middle East and North Africa during the seventh century was substantially different from the Islam with which we are now familiar. Rules such as that prohibiting images and the cross apparently did not then exist. And there is good reason to believe that the Qur'an, as we now know it, had not yet appeared — and would not appear until the middle of the eighth century.

That Islam was deeply indebted to Judaism and (to a much lesser extent) Christianity has of course always been understood. The whole of the Qur'an is full of references to well-known biblical characters such as Adam, Noah, Abraham, Moses, and Jesus. Muslims accept all of the Old Testament as divinely revealed scripture and hold Jesus to be a great prophet. Islamic tradition speaks of the "Last Days" when the "Antichrist" will appear and when Jesus will return to judge mankind and destroy evildoers. But the more we investigate the faith, the more thoroughly rooted in Judaism or Judeo-Christianity it appears. As Spencer notes, the earliest references to the followers of what we now call Islam by non-Muslims do not use the term "Muslim" or "Islam" at all, but instead speak of "Ishmaelites," "Hagarians," "Taiyaye," or "Saracens." The first two of these names are biblical, and indeed Islamic cultural vocabulary owes little to Arabia: There is scarcely a trace of native Arabian tradition in either the Qur'an or the hadiths. In the words of Arthur Jeffery, "the cultural vocabulary of the Qur'an is of non-Arabic origin."[1] He continues, "From the fact that Muhammad was an Arab, brought up in the midst of Arabian paganism and practising its rites himself until well on in manhood, one would naturally have expected to find that Islam had its roots deep down in this old Arabian paganism. It comes, therefore, as no little surprise, to find how little of the religious life of this Arabian paganism is reflected in the pages of the Qur'an."[2] Indeed, so little of Islam can be traced to Arabia that Luxenberg and several other commentators have suggested that we should seek its origins in the border regions of Israel and Syria.

---

1   Arthur Jeffery, *The Foreign Vocabulary of the Qur'an* (Oriental Institute Baroda, Vadodara, India, 1938), http://www.answering-islam.org/Books/Jeffrey/Vocabulary/intro.htm
2   Ibid.

Islam's cultural roots are in fact almost entirely Judaic. The Torah, the first five books of the Bible, which are said to have been written by Moses, are accepted completely as divine revelation. And the laws outlined in the Torah, especially in Leviticus and Deuteronomy, find their precise equivalents in Islamic law. Indeed the Jewish origins of Islamic moral and temporal law are well known and obvious. The strict monotheism of the Torah is matched by that of the Qur'an. The divine injunction to conquer the Promised Land found in the Torah is matched by the divine injunction of the Qur'an to conquer the world for Islam. Laws concerning divorce and adultery are identical in both religions. Both have circumcision. Even laws governing food are the same, with the same foods proscribed and permitted and the same method of slaughter recommended.

All of this leads to the suspicion that "Islam" was in origin a sect of Judaism, and this was the position adopted in the mid-twentieth century by Patricia Crone and Michael Crook.[1] However, since Islam also honors Jesus, or Isa, then the purely Judaic origin of the faith was called into question, and several writers, among them Günter Lüling and Christoph Luxenberg, proposed instead that it grew out of a Jewish branch of Christianity. We know in fact that several Judaizing sects of Christianity existed from the first century. These basically regarded Jesus as an orthodox Jew and demanded their followers accept the Law of Moses. The best known of such groups was, as we saw, that of the Ebionites or Nazarites. We know for certain that by the fifth century there existed large Nazarite communities throughout the Arabian Peninsula. Indeed, so prevalent were they that we may justifiably designate their beliefs as "Arab Christianity." Amongst them Jesus was accepted as the Messiah, but not the Son of God; he was the "messenger" of God, and was portrayed as a faithful follower of the Mosaic Code. The Gospels were not accepted as accurate accounts of the life of Jesus and other, alternative gospels were used instead.

In short, centuries before the supposed life of the prophet Muhammad there seems to have existed within Arabia a thriving religious movement which might be described as "proto-Islam."

The Ebionites were strongly Jewish, and Judaism in its origins was a militant faith. Throughout the first centuries B.C. and A.D., leaders claiming to be the Messiah appeared regularly among the Jews, stirring up ruinous rebellions against the power of Rome. The idea that the Messiah would be a military commander was central to Jewish religious ideas of the time.

---

1   Patricia Crone and Michael Cook, *Hagarism: The Making of the Islamic World* (Cambridge University Press, 1977)

A peaceful and suffering Messiah did not figure in their thinking. Even the disciples of Jesus, after his crucifixion, are said to have asked him when he would restore the kingdom of Israel to independence.

It is highly likely that these attitudes were shared by the Ebionites, who thus adhered to most of the beliefs and practices we now consider "Muslim." Islamic tradition itself admits that the Ebionite Christians of Arabia were among the first and most fervent followers of the new faith, and the Arab historians name an Ebionite monk, Waraqah ibn Nawfal, as one of the earliest converts to Islam.[1]

But even admitting the strongly Jewish tone of Ebionitism or proto-Islam, how are we to account for the transformation of the Christian Jesus — the "honored one" or "Muhammad" among the Ebionites — into the warlike prophet of the Islamic Qur'an? The answer to this, I believe, is found in the identity of the names "Jesus" and "Joshua." In English, of course, these two look quite different; in Hebrew, they are one and the same Yahoshua. "Jesus" is the English of the Greek transliteration of "Yahoshua" via Latin. Now Jesus of the New Testament may have been a pacifist, but Joshua of the Old Testament was anything but. It was he who led the Israelite tribes after the death of Moses and traveled with them across the River Jordan (from Arabia, no less) into the land of Canaan. In Canaan he prosecuted a war of extermination against the natives. In doing so, we are told, he was carrying out a divine injunction. The Arabs of the sixth and seventh centuries were almost entirely illiterate. In the minds of illiterates, stories from one part of a book are easily conflated with stories from another. Since the Ebionite faith in any case stressed obedience to the Law of Moses, in its entirety (with such injunctions as "an eye for an eye and a tooth for a tooth" and the stoning of women to death for adultery), and since they also held that Jesus commanded obedience to these laws, it would have been the easiest thing in the world to confuse Jesus with Joshua, who also, remember, was an obedient follower of the Mosaic Code. And this surmise is startlingly confirmed by the fact that in the Qur'an Maryam, the mother of Isa (Jesus), is the sister of Moses and Aaron. In other words, it is beyond question that Islam has confused and conflated events of the Bible which are in fact separated from each other by many centuries.

What then of the origins of the Qur'an, the holy book supposed by Muslims to have been given to Muhammad by the Angel Gabriel?

---

1 Martin Lings, *Muhammad: His Life Based on the Earliest Sources* (Suhail Academy Co.)

Anyone who has read the Muslim holy book will recognize at once that it is a puzzling document. It is not a story or a narrative in the normal sense, but a series of apparently unrelated incidents and statements. Muslims themselves only understand the Qur'an by allusion to the Hadith, an enormous collection of "traditions" about the life of Muhammad which incidentally explain the obscure events and statements of the Qur'an. The hadiths, however, did not begin to appear until around a century after the supposed date of Muhammad's death, and it is well-known that there existed for several centuries a veritable industry of hadith composition. Muslim scholars themselves admit that the vast majority of these were fakes. It would appear that the Abbasid Caliphs sponsored the production of hadiths during the eighth and ninth centuries for political reasons. Numerous of these hadiths actually contradict each other in treating of one and the same statement of the Qur'an.

But even with the help of the hadiths, the Qur'an remains a strange and puzzling text. Whole sentences and paragraphs seem to make no sense at all. Philologist Ger-R. Puin expressed a typical opinion when he stated that "every fifth sentence or so [of the Qur'an] simply doesn't make sense." Why? Could it be that it was originally composed in a language other than Arabic and imperfectly transcribed into the latter tongue? That is increasingly the position adopted by the scholarly community; and the suspicion is greatly strengthened by the discovery that "the names in the Qur'an consistently show signs of having been derived from Syriac."[1] Syriac was the ancient language of large parts of the Middle East, a dialect of Aramaic, which had been the *lingua franca* of the region since the time of the Achaemenid Persian Empire. Syriac is closely related to Arabic, but sufficiently different to cause confusion if not properly understood. The deeper scholars have examined the Qur'an, the more clear its Syriac roots have become. Whole passages and incidents which have defied the best efforts of scholars throughout the centuries to comprehend suddenly make perfect sense if read as Syriac. Thus for example in Qur'an 19:24 we read: "Then (one) cried unto her from below her, saying: Grieve not! Thy Lord hath placed a rivulet beneath thee." It is unclear from the text who is speaking, perhaps the newborn Jesus or someone else; and the significance of the "rivulet" is utterly puzzling. However, read as a Syriac text we find that it refers to the Virgin Birth of Jesus. Thus the infant Jesus — who speaks elsewhere in the Qur'an — tells Mary: "Do not be sad, your Lord has made your delivery legitimate."

---

1 Spencer, *Did Muhammad Exist?* op cit., p. 155

Indeed, read as a Syriac document, the Qur'an not only loses its obscurity but is rapidly revealed as a Christian devotional text, or lectionary. That, at least, is the opinion of two of the greatest philologists in the field, Günter Lüling and Christoph Luxenberg. In the words of the latter, if Qur'an "really means lectionary, then one can assume that the Koran intended itself first of all to be understood as nothing more than a liturgical book with selected texts from the *Scriptures* (the Old and New Testament) and not at all as a substitute for the *Scriptures* themselves."[1] Even events which have traditionally been understood by Muslims as referring to crucial events of the life of Muhammad reveal themselves, upon transcription into Syriac, as events of the life of Jesus. In the words of Robert Spencer,

> Many of the Qur'an's more obscure passages begin to make sense when read in the light of having a foundation in Christian theology. For example, there is an enigmatic sura on the Night of Power, *al-Qadr* ("Power") [the night when Muhammad supposedly received the Qur'an from the Angel Gabriel]: 'Behold, We sent it down on the Night of Power; and what shall teach thee what is the Night of Power? The Night of Power is better than a thousand months; in it the angels and the Spirit descend, by the leave of their Lord, upon every command. Peace it is, till the rising of dawn' (97:1-5). Muslims associate the Night of Power with the first appearance of Gabriel to Muhammad and the first revelation of the Qur'an; they commemorate this night during the fasting month of Ramadan. But the Qur'an makes no explicit connection between the Night of Power and the revelation of the Qur'an. The book doesn't explain what the Night of Power is, except to say it is the night on which the angels (not just one angel) and the Spirit descend and proclaim Peace.
>
> In the light of the Qur'an's Syriac Christian roots, there is another possible interpretation — that sura 97 refers to Christmas.
>
> The Qur'anic scholar Richard Bell saw in the night, angels, Spirit, and peace of the sura a hint of the Nativity even without a detailed philological examination: "The origin of the idea of the Night of Power is unexplained. The only other passage in the Quran which has any bearing on it is XLIV, 2a, 3. In some ways what is here said of it suggests that some account of the Eve of the Nativity may have given rise to it."
>
> Luxenberg points out that because the Night of Power is associated with the revelation of the Qur'an, Muslims undertook vigils during Ramadan. "However," he notes, "with regard to the history of religions this fact is all the more remarkable since Islam does not have a nocturnal liturgy (apart from the *tarawih*, prayers offered during the nights of Ramadan). There is thus every reason to think that

---

1 Ibid., p. 166

these vigils corresponded originally to a Christian liturgical practice connected to the birth of Jesus Christ, and which was later adopted by Islam, but re-interpreted by Islamic theology to mean the descent of the Koran."

A close textual analysis supports this argument. *Al-qadr*, the Arabic word for "power," also means "fate" or "destiny." Luxenberg observes that the Syriac *qaaf-daal-raa* — the *q-d-r* root of the Arabic word *al-qadr* — has three meanings, designating "i) the birth (meaning the moment of birth); ii) the star under which one is born and which determines the fate of the newly born; iii) The Nativity, or Christmas." He continues: "Thus defined, the term *al-qadr*, 'destiny,' is related to the star of birth, which the Koranic *al qadr* applies, in the context of this sura, to the Star of Christmas. As a result, a connection is found to be established with Matthew II.2, 'Saying, Where is he that is born King of the Jews? For we have seen his star in the East and are come to worship him.' " Then the verse "the Night of Power is better than a thousand months" (97:4) would be rendered "Christmas night is better than a thousand vigils."

The Qur'an concludes the Night of Power passage with "Peace it is, till the rising of dawn" (97:5). Luxenberg notes that this verse "sends us back to the hymn of the Angels cited by Luke II.14: 'Glory to God in the highest and on earth peace, good will toward men.' This chant of the Angels has always constituted the principal theme of the Syriac vigils of the Nativity which lasts into Christmas night, with all sorts of hymns, more than all the other vigils." Indeed, in the Syriac Orthodox Church, the Divine Liturgy of the Nativity was traditionally celebrated at dawn, after a nightlong vigil — "Peace it is, till the rising of dawn."[1]

If such crucial events of the Islamic faith as the Night of Power can so easily be interpreted in a Christian manner, we will not then be surprised to find that even the Qur'an's five references to "Muhammad" (the "chosen one" or "praised one") could equally well refer to Jesus as to any supposed Arabian prophet.

The evidence then, taken together, would then suggest that no Arabian prophet named Muhammad existed, and that "Muhammad" was originally a title of Jesus. This means that what we now call Islam did not exist until near the end of the seventh century or even into the first half of the eighth. What existed before was proto-Islam, a branch of the Arabian Christian sect otherwise known as Ebionitism.

From about the third century onwards we hear of "Saracens" raiding along the borders of the Roman Empire in Syria. It is true that these earlier Saracens cannot have been Ebionites or proto-Muslims, but it seems likely

---

1 Ibid., pp. 184-5

that the militaristic spirit of this cult would have appealed to the nomad Arabs. Certainly by the fourth and fifth centuries there are reports of Saracen groups ranging as far east as Mesopotamia (modern Iraq) that were involved in battles on both the Persian and Roman sides.[1] They are described in the Roman administrative document *Notitia dignitatum*—dating from the time of Theodosius I in the 4th century—as comprising distinctive units in the Roman army and they are distinguished in the document from other Arabs.[2]

TOWARDS A SOLUTION

It seems clear then that the entire narrative of early Islam, as it is now understood, from its origins to its initial expansion beyond the Arabian Peninsula, is an elaborate work of fiction put together in the late seventh and early eighth centuries. But if this be the case, if no man named Muhammad actually existed and if the Arab conquest of Persia is a myth, what then did happen? How are we to interpret the facts uncovered by archeology and by textual analysis?

In *Did Muhammad Exist?* Robert Spencer argues that the whole myth of Muhammad, as a separate person from Jesus, was invented by Arab propagandists between 700 and 730 in order to unify and justify the massive Arab empire that then existed. Although Spencer does not go into the question of how that empire came to exist in the first place, there are very good grounds for believing that it was not originally an Arab creation at all, and that the invention of an Arabian prophet as the spiritual fountain-head of this empire was motivated by a desire to justify what was essentially the Arab takeover of an imperial machine that was not theirs.

According to accepted ideas, immediately after Muhammad's death a series of Islamic leaders known as the *Rashidun* or "Rightly-guided Caliphs"— Abu Bakr, Umar, Uthman and Ali — began the conquest of a vast empire which would, within two decades or so, spread Muslim rule from Libya to the borders of India. The problem with this story is that archaeologists have found not a trace of these men. Not a brick, inscription, or artifact of any kind belonging to the "Rightly-guided Caliphs" has come to light. Archaeologically, they are as unattested as Muhammad himself — a circumstance which must naturally lead us to question their existence.

We recall at this point the thoroughly Persian character of early Islam — which certainly seems to indicate that the new faith took shape in an Iranian

---

1 Jan Retso, *The Arabs in Antiquity: Their History from the Assyrians to the Umayyads* (Rutledge and Kegan Paul, 2003), pp. 464-6
2 Ibid.

or at least a joint Arab–Iranian cultural context. This is further suggested by the fact that the appearance of Islam in Iran is not marked by a destruction layer, as in the Byzantine lands, which in turn indicates that Islam entered Iran peacefully and was adopted voluntarily by the Persians. As we saw earlier, there is some evidence to suggest that the Persian emperor Chosroes II embraced the new faith, or rather the Christian heresy (Ebionitism) which would later develop into the new faith. We know for a fact that he did indeed abandon Zoroastrianism. Shortly after ascending the throne he faced a rebellion from one of his generals, Bahram Chobin, who proclaimed himself King Bahram VI. In his hour of need Chosroes fled to the Byzantine emperor Maurice, who put an army at his disposal with which he regained the crown. This fostered a liberal attitude to Christianity, as did his marriage to the beautiful Shirin, a Christian apparently from Syria. The Persian emperor, we are told, embraced the religion of his favorite wife, though the sincerity of his faith was always suspect. Gibbon speaks of "the imaginary conversion of the king of Persia [to Christianity]," which "was reduced to a local and superstitious veneration for Sergius, one of the saints of Antioch, who heard his prayers and appeared to him in dreams."[1] But if Chosroes' conversion to Christianity was suspect, his behavior at Jerusalem, where he plundered the most sacred Christian relics and ordered the massacre of the city's Christian population, marks him out as a fanatic, and a very violent one at that. The evidence indicates that Chosroes remained a Christian, of sorts, but of a very different variety to that which pertained at Constantinople.

As Hugh Trevor-Roper so sagely noted, when one civilization converts to another's faith, it normally embraces a heresy of that faith:[2] thus the Roman Empire converted to a heresy of Judaism — Christianity — and it would appear that the Persian king and his people converted to a heresy of Christianity.

We are told that Chosroes' wife Shirin was a follower of the Nestorian branch of Christianity, though she is said to have later embraced the Syrian Miaphysite doctrine. Yet her exact beliefs are uncertain, and we may justifiably ask: Was it the Syrian Miaphysite Church or the Syrian Ebionite Church which Shirin, Chosroes' favorite wife, joined in later life? If it was the Ebionite (Arab Christian) Church, a faith doctrinally very close to Islam, and if Chosroes himself followed his wife into this sect, then a whole host of hitherto intractable puzzles and conundrums begin to solve themselves.

---

1 Gibbon, *Decline and Fall*, Chapter 46
2 Trevor-Roper, op cit., p. 57

To begin with, the astonishing narrative of the Arab conquests, which supposedly saw a few nomads on camels simultaneously attack and conquer the mighty Persian and Byzantine empires, is revealed as a fiction: it was the heavy cavalry of the Sassanid Persians which created the "Islamic" Empire. Secondly, the strange modesty of the "Rightly-guided" caliphs, Abu Bakr, Umar, and the others, in failing to leave a single coin or artifact bearing their names, is explained by the fact that they did not exist and were invented precisely to disguise the Arab usurpation of the Sassanid Empire. Thirdly, the "Islamic" coins of Chosroes II, a king who died supposedly over ten years before the Islamic conquest of Persia, are no longer a mystery and were minted not by a modest Arabian caliph but by Chosroes II himself. And finally, the failure of the poet Firdowsi to mention either a caliph named Umar or a prophet named Muhammad is fully explained, and the war described in the *Shahnameh* during Yazdegerd's reign was a civil war pitting Islamicized (or Ebionitized) Persians against Arabs.

Huge numbers of Arab troops and irregular fighters had apparently accompanied the Persians on their march of conquest throughout Syria, Egypt and North Africa. The outcome of the Persian or rather "Islamic" civil war which broke out in the time of Yazdegerd III was an Arab *coup d'état*: An Arab dynasty, under Mu'awyia (founder of the Ummayads), seized control of the Sassanid throne. They were able to do this at least partly because of Yazdegerd's unpopularity and because a majority of the Persian king's subjects were already Arabs, or at least Semite-speakers closely related culturally to the Arabs. The Persian kings themselves were mostly born and raised in Mesopotamia, a land whose Semitic language was very close to Arabic. Furthermore, the regions of the Middle East which they conquered were predominantly Syriac in speech.

But the Arab seizure of power led to a realignment and redefinition of the Ebionite (Arab Christian) faith. A new creation myth, as it were, was needed. Hence, during the time of Abd al-Malik (d. 705) and of his son Al Walid, the last vestiges of Persian influence were removed from the coinage, and Arabic became the official language of the court at Damascus. Along with these measures, it became expedient to "Arabize" the faith, with the invention of an Arabic alphabet and an Arabian prophet quite different from the original *muhammad* (Jesus). It was then too that the story of an Arab conquest of Persia and the Middle East was invented, along with the conquering caliphs, Abu Bakr and Umar, who supposedly carried it out.

If the above narrative is correct, if neither Muhammad nor the "Rightly-guided" conquering caliphs existed, and if it was the Persians who created the "Islamic" (or rather Arab "Christian") Empire, this implies that the dates found in Chosroes II's, Yazdegerd's and Mu'awiya's coins, which have hitherto been assumed to be Age of Hegira years, have nothing whatsoever to do with Muhammad's *hijra* and must instead commemorate some event of Persian history. It should be noted that no inscription on any of these early coins actually says "Age of Hegira". On some coins, however, the date is followed by the explanation "in the age of following the Arabs"; in short, when the Persian kings converted to an Arab sect or religious group. Clearly, if Chosroes II was first to do this, and if his conversion to Arab Christianity was influenced by his wife Shirin, then this could have occurred as early as 590.

The term Age of Hegira actually only appears on Islamic coins from the eleventh century onwards, when it is generally written in conjunction with the *anno domini* date of the Christians. The two appear on coins side by side. From this it would appear that all the so-called Age of Hegira dates found on Islamic coins generally dated between the seventh and early eleventh centuries do not refer to the Hegira of Muhammad, and that successive Muslim rulers changed the dating system arbitrarily on more than one occasion. This latter is suggested by the discovery of Islamic coins of wildly differing dates in sites and strata of the same epoch. It was only in the conventional eleventh century (Illig's eighth century) that the Arab Christian (by now fully Islamic) world adopted a calendar supposedly deriving from an event in the life of Muhammad.

However, creating an Arab prophet named "Muhammad" was one thing (and it is admitted that a whole industry existed fabricating hadiths supposedly describing this man's life), but how did they determine when he lived? As we saw earlier, Illig holds that it cannot be coincidence that precisely 297 years elapsed between the Council of Nicea (325), when Ebionitism was declared a heresy and its followers retreated in Arabia, and 622, the year in which Muhammad is supposed to have fled from Mecca to Medina (the Hegira). For other reasons entirely Illig has identified the number of phantom years added to the calendar as 297 — though the present writer believes 300 to be the more accurate figure.

In any event, one way or another, the Muslims followed the Christians in inserting about three hundred phantom years into the calendar, and a prophet "Muhammad" was made to live three centuries before the actual spread of Arab Christianity or proto-Islam throughout the Middle East and North Africa. Having adopted the European take on chronology, the Arab chroniclers then proceeded to fill their phantom centuries just as the Europeans did theirs: by duplicating and triplicating existing kings and dynasties and placing them in chronological sequence. Thus Spain's Abd' er Rahman III, of the tenth century, was duplicated in Abd' er Rahman II, of the ninth century and triplicated as Abd' er Rahman I of the eighth. And the same process was followed at the other end of the Muslim world. In this way Mahmud (Mohammed) of Ghazni, the Muslim conqueror of northern India at the start of the eleventh century found his alter-ego in Mohammed bin Qasim, Muslim conqueror of northern India at the beginning of the eighth century. An identical process can be discerned throughout the Arab world, and there is evidence that the custom of multiplying king-lists and dynasties was not simply copied from the Europeans: as early as 1964 Jan Ryckmans remarked on the profound confusion created in the pre-Islamic history of southern Arabia by the deliberate duplication and triplication of kings and king-lists in that part of the world.[1]

---

1 Jan Ryckmans, "La chronologie des rois de Saba et Du-Raydan," *Journal of the Netherlands Institute for the Near East*, Vol. 16 (1964)

CHAPTER 5: RECONSTRUCTING THE SEVENTH CENTURY

THE SEVENTH CENTURY RENAISSANCE

It is impossible to overstate the impact of Illig's system on our view of Europe's history. For one thing, the elimination of the Dark Age centuries from the calendar means also the elimination of the Dark Age as a cultural epoch. If Illig is right, far from signaling the commencement of a Dark Age, the seventh century actually saw the beginning of the most dramatic expansion, growth, and technological change the West had ever experienced. Historians have long recognized that the great wave of new technologies and ideas, most coming from the Far East, which transformed Europe in the Middle Ages, is strangely divided into two separate phases; one beginning in the sixth and early seventh centuries, and the other beginning in the latter tenth century. The earlier phase of this phenomenon saw, in the sixth century, the introduction to Europe of silk production and the stirrup. The latter technology revolutionized warfare and arrived in the West at roughly the same time as the secrets of silk, via the good offices of the Avars. It seems that double-masted ships, able to sail into the wind, likewise made their first appearance in Byzantine waters from the end of the sixth century.

We know that during the sixth century the Byzantines and even the western Europeans were also active innovators in their own right. The moldboard plow, which enabled the inhabitants of temperate Europe to break in the heavy damp soils of those regions, spread rapidly throughout the fifth and sixth centuries. The horseshoe may have appeared at this time too. In Byzantium, natural philosophers made important advances in a whole host of technical and theoretical fields of knowledge. Astronomical clocks using advanced cog-wheel systems were created, and important advances were made in the fields of medical science and astronomy. According to Professor Samuel Sambursky, the researches of the Byzantine scholars of the sixth century were anticipating, in many ways, the discoveries of the Renaissance and the Enlightenment. By the sixth century, he shows, Neo-Platonic philosophers were constructing complex machines using cog-wheel technology, as well as making important discoveries about the natural world.[1]

Even music was revolutionized at this time, with the appearance of the violin and perhaps also the bagpipe, in Byzantium, instruments which solved the problem of tonal discontinuity.

Then, according to conventional ideas, came three centuries of darkness and depopulation, after which the torch of technological and scientific innovation was again taken up by the peoples of the West. As we saw, attempts to explain this depopulation and darkness as a consequence of natural catastrophe or human action have proved unsatisfactory. It is true, of course, as Henri Pirenne pointed out, that the arrival of the Arabs (or the Islamicized Persians and Arabs) on the scene in the second decade of the seventh century undoubtedly caused much disruption and put a damper on things for a while. It was without question the Arab/Persian conquests which reduced the great Roman cities of the Middle East and North Africa to ruins and which left their hinterlands barren deserts. Saracen slave-raiding along the southern shores of Europe likewise forced an abrupt abandonment of the old Roman settlement patterns, with their scattered and undefended villas. Archeology shows that in the second or third decade of the seventh century populations moved quickly to defended hilltops — the first medieval castles.[2] And Arab piracy closed the Mediterranean to trade — except of course the slave-trade conducted by the Arabs themselves. The flow of papyrus, essential for a literate and urban civilization, was terminated. Pirenne was absolutely right to state that the seventh century saw Europe thrown back on her own resources and cut off from the fountains of high civilization to the East. But this did not, as Pirenne imagined, produce a Dark Age. Some of the more refined features of classical Roman civilization, it is true, disappeared. Termination of the Mediterranean trade meant that many luxuries such as spices and wines became unavailable in Europe. The burgeoning Merovingian glass industry declined and died as the high-quality soda from

---

1 Samuel Sambursky, *The Physical World of Late Antiquity* (Routledge and Kegan Paul, 1962)

2 Hodges and Whitehouse, op cit., pp. 44-8

the eastern Mediterranean, necessary for the production of fine glass, became unavailable. But it is wrong to imagine that every feature of classical civilization disappeared, or that Europe entered anything resembling a Dark Age. Thrown onto their own resources, the native inventiveness of the continent's inhabitants now came into its own, as local substitutes for things previously imported were sought and found. Furthermore, the flow of new ideas from the Far East, from India and China, which had commenced in the sixth century, did not now grind to a halt, in spite of Arab piracy. Some of the new ideas may thereby have been delayed, but they were not canceled.

When the flow of new technologies and ideas to the West is resumed, in the (conventional) tenth century, they arrived via the filter of the Arabs. But, as we saw earlier, even this has created an enormous problem for conventional scholarship. Why, it has been asked, did the cultural and ideological impact of Islam and the Arabs make itself felt in Europe only in the tenth and eleventh centuries, whereas it should have been expected in the seventh? With the Dark Age centuries removed, however, everything makes sense, and the arrival in the West, through the Islamicized Middle East, of paper-making, "Arabic" numerals, windmills, and a host of other revolutionary technologies, would not then have occurred in the tenth century as per convention but in the second half of the seventh.

Illig's system thus reveals that the Europeans were not at all slow learners; they adopted new ideas and technologies from the Arabs very quickly indeed. It is true, as Pirenne pointed out, that the Arabs did not bequeath these things to the Europeans voluntarily, and it is equally true that their raiding and pillaging may have slightly impeded or delayed the introduction to Europe of some of them. But the delay was short. A new technology or idea can be transmitted to another society by a single individual: it does not need regular trade or economic contact. Such contact, in a limited way (in the form of the slave trade) did actually exist, but even if it hadn't, the new technologies would have reached Europe, and done so with great speed. We know that Jewish refugees from the Muslim conquests brought several crucial innovations to Europe, amongst them apparently "Arabic" numerals.

With the "Dark" centuries removed, we now find that during the seventh century Europe's population, which had begun to revive with the Christianization of the continent in the fifth and sixth centuries, continued to expand. The long centuries of demographic decline, which characterized pagan Rome (and Greece), came to an end. Following the biblical injunction to "be fruitful and multiply and fill the earth," the Christians and their Jewish cousins alone enjoyed naturally increasing populations during the second to fifth centuries. The revival came first in the East, which had been Christianized first. The great cities of the Byzantine Empire of the fifth and sixth centuries surpassed in size and opulence anything seen under the Caesars. The West was Christianized later, but when it was, the impact was the same as in the East. Spain, the earliest region of the West to become Christian, was also first to enjoy a natural increase in population, an increase discernible under the Visigoths, during the fifth and sixth centuries. The population of Gaul also began to grow again, for the first time in four centuries. The revival in Britain and Germany began somewhat later, as they were converted to Christianity later, but from the sixth and early seventh centuries the populations of both regions began to expand.

This was the picture when Islam burst upon the scene in the early seventh century. The closing of the Mediterranean to normal trade after that time certainly put a damper on the European revival — for a few decades, anyhow. The educated laity which characterized antique Roman civilization disappeared, along with the libraries and the papyrus upon which the works of the Greek and Roman authors were written. There was a certain degree of cultural impoverishment, and the church became almost the sole custodian of the intellectual legacy of Greece and Rome.

Yet this "dim" period, which must have endured for several decades, was by no means anything like the "Dark Age" envisaged by historians for over a thousand years. Towns continued to expand, after the centuries of contraction under the Romans, and new commercial centers were developed, as the economic center of gravity in Europe shifted from the Mediterranean towards the north. Historians are agreed that a major revival of towns began in the latter tenth century, which is, of course, in Illig's system, the latter seventh. Some of these were located around ecclesiastical foundations, and the church became a major engine of this revival, a revival which saw the reestablishment of the Western Roman Empire, though now under German leadership. Otto I's crowning would, under the new chronology, have occurred in 662, not 962, and would have been directly inspired by the collapse of Byzantine power (and therefore Constantinople's claims in the West) in the face of the Arab onslaught.

RECONNECTING THE STRANDS

In theory, bridging the gap between the two real historical epochs, the seventh and tenth centuries, should be simple enough; and we might expect a straightforward continuation of events and characters from August 614 through to September 911 (in Illig's estimate) and beyond. This has generally been the case with the ancient, pre-Christian histories of Egypt and Mesopotamia, whose chronologies have been examined by various researchers over the past few decades. However, with the medieval Dark Age things are not so simple, as Illig himself has emphasized. The mistakes in pre-Christian history were largely (though not entirely) accidental; so, in general, there should be a straightforward progression of events once "dark ages" are removed. With the medieval Dark Age, there seems to have been a concerted effort on the part of the church and imperial authorities to provide a "history" for the three non-existent centuries. The result, as we saw in chapter 3, was a proliferation of forged chronicles and documents of every kind, most of which were created in German and French monasteries between the eleventh and fourteenth centuries. These forgeries, which covered the three dark centuries and reached well into the "real" time of the tenth century, were produced by some extremely erudite men, and often, as we have noted, used real characters and events with which to "fill out" the non-existent time.

Illig's take on this question is rather different, and he tends to assume that all the characters and events between 614 and 911 are entirely fictitious. It is evident that this cannot be the case. There is no question, for example, that the Persian conquest of Egypt, in 619-620 really occurred, and there seems little reason to doubt that it occurred pretty much as the surviving accounts claim. Indeed, the Sassanid invasion of Egypt is probably the last major action of the seventh century which we can be reasonably sure occurred when it is said to have occurred. As such, 620 would probably be a better date than 614 as a marker for the commencement of the phantom time-frame. Such being the case, we might be tempted to expect everything between 620 and 920 to be fictitious — but again things are not quite so simple. We have seen, for example, that in Persia there is abundant evidence for the existence not only of Chosroes II but of his successors right up to Yazdegered III; and there is clear proof that the early Ummayad Caliphs, from Mu'awiya right through to Al-Walid, were real people who have left substantial archaeological proof of their existence. Thus the "phantom time" period cannot have commenced in the Persian and Arab world until near the end of the seventh century — though on the other hand events of the early seventh century and even the late sixth, such as the life of Muhammad and the conquests of the "Rightly-guided" caliphs Abu Bakr and Umar — are revealed to be typically fictitious inventions of the phantom Dark Age.

And things are no less complicated in the West. Archaeological finds confirm that in the Frankish lands the reign of Clothair II, a contemporary of Heraclius, was a period of some prosperity and expansion; and there seems little reason to doubt that he reigned until 629, as the written histories maintain. Furthermore, there are good grounds for believing that his son Dagobert I, who is said to have reigned until 634, was a real enough person. Thus in the Merovingian territories we might be tempted to commence the period of phantom time with the death of Dagobert I, and to pronounce everything after that date as fictitious. Again, however, things are not quite so simple: there are good grounds for believing that several of the Frankish rulers placed in the eighth and ninth centuries were historical characters. We see the same problem in England. Here archaeological evidence confirms the existence of well-known Dark Age characters such as Offa of Mercia and Alfred the Great. Both these latter must have been contemporaneous with the Vikings, whose raids, we have seen, can only have commenced around 640. (That Offa is said to have predated the Vikings, though he copied the design of evidently Viking-supplied Islamic gold coins, is a spectacular proof of the absurdity of accepted chronology).[1]

It is evident, then, that in our attempts to untie the Gordion Knot of seventh/eighth century history we must proceed with extreme caution.

The most outstanding character to emerge from the pages of the Dark Age chronicles is of course Charlemagne, and Illig has gone to great lengths to illustrate that he is an entirely mythical being. In his *Das erfundene Mittelalter* he has demonstrated in detail that virtually all of the architectural structures attributed to his time — most especially the Chapel at Aachen — reveal themselves to be, on closer inspection, monuments of the eleventh century. Illig, as we saw in Chapter 3, has emphasized that the whole cult of Charles the Great was a creation of the Ottonian emperors of the tenth century, and he has argued that the great emperor is nothing but a creation of the Ottonian scribes, called to life for propaganda purposes; the chief one of which was to provide a precedent for a German monarch donning the imperial purple of a Roman Emperor.

As we saw earlier, however, there is every likelihood that the "historical" Charlemagne was based upon an actual Germanic king of the fifth or sixth century, and there are one or two very likely candidates. Gunnar Heinsohn as well as H. E. Korth and several others have stressed parallels between the great Ostrogothic king Theodoric, who ruled the whole of Italy as well as

---

1 One tradition preserved among the Hungarians of Transylvania insists that Arpad, first king of the Magyars, was a descendant of Attila the Hun. The two are separated by five generations, just over a century. This strongly implies that Arpad and the Hungarians arrived in central Europe in the middle of the sixth century — precisely contemporary with the arrival of the Avars.

parts of Gaul and southern Germany during the late fifth and early sixth centuries, and Charlemagne.[1] There is no question that Theodoric was a figure of immense importance in his time and could easily be seen as a worthy candidate for a prototype German Emperor. He entered Teutonic legend as King Dietrich and medieval German tradition attributed to him a series of wholly fabulous achievements. That said, his actual deeds were not unimpressive, and there seems little doubt that the figure of Charlemagne was at least partly based upon him. However, Theodoric was not a Frank but an Ostrogoth, whereas Charlemagne was very definitely a king of the Franks. Such being the case, it seems likely that the *persona* of Charlemagne was mainly based on the Frankish king Theodebert I, whose assistance the emperor Justinian sought against the Ostrogoths during the Italian wars in the 550s. We know that after the defeat of the Ostrogoths Justinian's forces came into conflict with their Frankish allies. Theodebert I successfully made war against the Byzantines for several years and seemed to revel in his newfound power and prestige. A rumour even spread in Constantinople that he intended to invade Thrace. Symbolic of his prestige he then took the unprecedented step of issuing coins bearing his own image, an action bewailed by the Byzantine historian Procopius, who saw in it a presage to the final breakup of the Roman Empire.

It is highly likely that the great warrior who minted coins of himself dressed as a Roman emperor was none other than Theodebert I. He too, like the Charlemagne admired by the Ottonians, was a Frank, and he preceded Otto I (if Illig is right) by just over a century, as did Charlemagne, according to conventional dating.

From all of this it is clear that the real history of the seventh (or conventional tenth) century is as yet a closed book, and any attempts to open and read the pages of that book will need to be made with extreme care. However, alongside the plethora of "histories" and chronicles which already exist for the seventh and tenth centuries, and which undoubtedly contain some real history, we also have a new and powerful body of evidence not available to previous generations — that of archeology.

I hope, in the pages to follow, to utilize both types of evidence and to try to find, where possible, a coming together of the two.

Before beginning, however, we need to outline a few general principles and guidelines. First and foremost, as we noted earlier, even as things stand,

---

1 See H. E. Korth, www.jahr1000wen.de

there is surprising agreement, in general terms, between the histories of the seventh and tenth centuries. Thus in the early seventh century Italy found herself under the dominion of the Langobards, a tribe of Germanic barbarians which had arrived in the peninsula in the late sixth century; whilst in the early tenth century Italy found herself controlled by the supposed descendants of the Langobards, who now appear under the name "Lombards."

The Langobards had been pushed westwards into Italy by a nomadic people of the steppes named the Avars, speakers of an Ural-Altaic dialect apparently related to the language of the Huns. By the early seventh century the Avars, ensconced in the Hungarian Plain, were making raids deep into the territories of the Franks, then ruled by the Merovingian kings. In the same way, by the early tenth century another tribe of Ural-Altaic speakers, the Magyars, were stationed in the Hungarian Plain and from there making raids deep into the territories of the Franks, this time ruled by the so-called Carolingian kings.

This alone would suggest that the Magyars and the Avars were one and the same people, and would finally make sense of the strong tradition among the Hungarians that they are descents of, or at least relatives of, the Huns. Conventional scholarship, of course, has always viewed this claim with extreme scepticism, due to the long stretch of time supposedly separating the arrival in the west of the Magyars from the arrival of the Huns and Avars.

And whilst on this topic we should note that the removal of the three Dark Age centuries also casts new light on the history of the Magyars' neighbors, the Romanians. Historians have long struggled to find a material connection between the Latin-speaking population of Roman Dacia and the medieval Vlachs, whose Latin-based language is strikingly similar to modern Italian. In conventional terms a huge stretch of time separates the last Roman colony of Dacia (abandoned in the third century) from the first appearance of the Romanian-speaking Vlachs in the eleventh century. If, however, the eleventh century is really the eighth then the span of time between Roman Dacia and the medieval Vlachs is not too great. Indeed, since the lands to the immediate south of Dacia, ancient Maesia (modern Bulgaria), were part of the Roman Empire until the latter sixth century, then the survival of Latin-speaking populations throughout the whole Balkans region into the medieval age (seventh-eighth century), becomes perfectly logical. The advance of the Avars and Slavs into Maesia shortly after 600 can only have caused massive disruption to the Latin-speaking farmers and townsfolk of the region, great numbers of whom seem to have sought refuge in wooded and mountainous terrain. The Transylvanian hills were then, as now, relatively remote and inaccessible, and would have offered an ideal retreat for the uprooted and terrified Romans. Other mountainous parts of the Balkans also received Latin-speaking refugees, evidence of which is found in the small Vlach or Romanian-speaking populations of Bulgaria, Serbia, and Greece which survive to this day.

It was Otto I who broke the power of the Magyars at the Battle of Lechfeld, the same Otto I who proclaimed himself Emperor of the West in 955 (in reality 655, according to the revised chronology). But if Otto I actually reigned in the first half of the seventh century, this would imply that he was a scion of the Frankish Merovingian dynasty, and such being the case it is clear that Frankish Carolingians of the tenth century must be identical, in some way or other, with the Merovingians of the seventh.

SEVENTH CENTURY MEROVINGIANS AND TENTH CENTURY CAROLINGIANS

Any student of early medieval history is at once struck by the obvious parallels between the seventh and tenth centuries in the lands of the Franks. So for example in France, by the first quarter of the seventh century, the unity of the Merovingian realms, always precarious in the first place, was beginning to unravel. We hear how King Dagobert I (629–634) appointed his son Sigebert III as ruler of the eastern territories — the predominantly Germanic-speaking regions that would later become a separate state and nation. In the same way, in the early tenth century, the Carolingian state was divided into a French west and a German east when the Frankish ruler of Saxony, Henry the Fowler (Heinrich der Vögler), established his own independent German kingdom.

Historians note also that the Carolingian kings of tenth century France bear typically Merovingian names, though in somewhat updated form. Thus, as we saw in Chapter 2, Louis, a common name amongst tenth century monarchs, is simply the Merovingian Clovis — minus the initial "c" (Louis is written as Lovis in Latin), whilst Lothair, another tenth century king's name, is the Merovingian Clothair, again minus the initial "c." This knowledge might lead us to the conclusion that all we need do, to produce a real or "joined-up" history of the seventh/tenth century is match seventh century Merovingian kings with tenth century Carolingians. Unfortunately, things are not quite so straightforward. The two lines do not "fit" in the sense that neither the names of the kings nor their life stories can be made to agree with each other. If we assume that all the Merovingians up to Clothair II (584–629) were real people, we must admit, along with Illig, that fictitious persons and events follow. Clothair II himself is well attested in archaeological remains of various kinds, as is his son Dagobert I, who apparently reigned until 634. Beyond that, we enter the archaeological "dark age," from which almost nothing has emerged.

So much for the seventh century: At the other end of the scale, in the tenth century, it is just that part of the century — the first quarter or third — which is most secure with regard to the Merovingians, that is most questionable with regard to their Carolingian successors. Thus the tenth century is said to have been ushered in by the reign of a very weak king called Charles ("the Simple"), who in 911 bequeathed a large part of northern France — henceforth called Normandy — to a group of Viking raiders under Rollo. Applying Illig's rule of subtracting 297 (or 300) years from all dates of the tenth century onwards, this would place the coming of the Normans in 614. However, for a large number of reasons it is clear that this event could not have occurred so early. As we saw earlier, the Scandinavian expansion was intimately connected with the rise of Islam: the Muslim demand for European slaves and concubines was met by the Vikings, who were primarily slave-raiders and traders. These the Vikings supplied mainly through raids into Russia, but also through expeditions to the West. According to conventional ideas such raids began shortly before 800 — about 150 years after the rise of Islam. Yet, as we have noted, there is much evidence (for example that of Islamic coins) to suggest that the Viking expansion actually commenced in the middle of the seventh century. Since the earliest Islamic coins found in Viking contexts belong to the mid-seventh century, we must assume that the Viking Age began around that time. Adding on the three phantom centuries to our chronology, this would place the beginning of real Carolingian history also in the middle of the tenth century. Rollo's Vikings would perchance then have been granted land in Normandy anywhere between 950 and 980, though probably closer to the latter.

We note here the existence of a Carolingian King Lothair IV, who is generally placed between 954 and 986. He may well be one and the same as the Merovingian Clothair III, who is said to have reigned between 639 and 673. We should note that almost nothing is known of the life of Lothair IV, whilst Clothair III is likewise a great unknown and is generally regarded as the first of *les rois fainéants*, the "do-nothing kings." It is likely then that from the time of Clothair III onwards seventh century "Merovingian" history should be ignored, and we should look instead to tenth century Carolingian history.

As we have seen, the death of Clothair II in 629 signaled the final breakup of a unified Merovingian state, and we know that Clothair II's son, Dagobert I, appointed Sigebert III, the latter only a child, as ruler of the eastern Frankish territories, the regions which would in future form the German lands of the Holy Roman Empire. We know that Sigebert III's appointment as ruler of the east was mainly to satisfy the Austrasian aristocracy, who exercised a certain degree of autonomy. On the death of Dagobert, Sigebert ruled Austrasia independently, and under the tutelage of Blessed Pepin of Landen and other saints of the time, the young king is said to have grown into pious adulthood. We hear that whilst still a boy Sigebert tried in vain to add Thuringia to his kingdom, but was defeated by Duke Radulph, supposedly in 640. The *Chronicle of Fredegar* records that the rout of his army left Sigebert weeping in his saddle. From this, it has been surmised that, at least in part, the downfall of the Merovingian dynasty was a result of child rule, for both Sigebert and his younger brother Clovis II, who ruled in Neustria, were prepubescent children who could not fight on the field and whose regents had their own interests at heart.

Radulph (died after 642), who defeated Sigebert III, was, according to the Chronicle of Fredegar, son of one Chamar, a Frankish aristocrat. Radulph rose to power under Dagobert I, who appointed him as *dux* in the former Thuringian kingdom which the Franks had conquered in 531. His installation was meant to protect the eastern border of the Frankish realm against the threatening Slavic Wends under Samo, who had defeated Dagobert I at the Battle of Wogastisburg in 631. Radulf fought successfully against the Slavs but subsequently refused to incorporate secured territories into the Austrasian kingdom. To retain his independence he allied with Fara, a descendant of the powerful Agilolfing dynasty in Bavaria who ruled over large estates along the River Main.

We are immediately drawn to compare the life of Radulph with that of Henry the Fowler, three hundred years later.

Henry the Fowler was born in Memleben, in what is now Saxony-Anhalt. He was the son of Otto the Illustrious, Duke of Saxony, and his wife Hedwiga, daughter of Henry of Franconia and Ingeltrude. Through Hedwiga, Henry claimed to be the great, great, great-grandson of Charlemagne.[1] Like Count Radulph, three centuries earlier, Henry presided over the separation of the German-speaking Frankish lands from the French-speaking regions to the west, and like Radulph, he spent much of his life battling against dangerous enemies to the east. We are told that the Hungarians began raiding

---

1 If Charlemagne or Carlus was the same person as Theodebert I (500–547), as the *Additamentum* to the Easter Tables of Victorius of Aquitaine would suggest, then Henry the Fowler would have flourished around the middle of the seventh century.

deep into Germany in 921. These attacks continued uninterruptedly until 926 when Henry, having captured a Hungarian prince, managed to arrange a ten-year-truce. Though still forced to pay tribute to the Magyars, this truce nevertheless gave the German lands time to fortify towns and train a new elite cavalry force.

We hear that during the truce with the Hungarians, Henry subdued the Polabian Slavs who had settled on the eastern border of his realm. In the winter of 928, he marched against the Slavic Hevelli tribes and seized their capital, Brandenburg. He then invaded the lands of the Glomacze on the middle Elbe River, conquered Gana (Jahna), the capital after a siege, and had a fortress (the later Albrechtsburg) built at Meissen. In 929, with the help of Arnulf of Bavaria, Henry entered Bohemia and forced Duke Wenceslaus I to resume the yearly payment of tribute to the king. Meanwhile, the Slavic Redarii had driven away their chief, captured the town of Walsleben and massacred the inhabitants. Counts Bernard and Thietmar marched against the fortress of Lenzen beyond the Elbe, and, after fierce fighting, completely routed the enemy in September 929. The Lusatians and the Ukrani on the lower Oder were subdued and made tributary in 932 and 934, respectively.

Both Henry and Radulph therefore spent much of their lives fighting against Ural-Altaic-speaking nomads stationed on the Hungarian Plain (Magyars and Avars) and against Slavic tribes infiltrating German territories along the Elbe and the borders of Bavaria, and both inaugurated an epoch of independence for the eastern territories of the Franks. This is not, however, to suggest that Henry the Fowler and Duke Radulph were one and the same person. It is likely that the latter character is a fictitious invention of the eleventh/twelfth century monks who fabricated the histories of the three dark centuries. He was almost certainly a duplicate of an earlier potentate of the same name from the sixth century. This earlier Radulph was also contemporary with a prince named Sigebert, this time Sigebert I, and the latter character seems unquestionably to have formed the prototype of Sigebert III, the supposed son of Dagobert I of the seventh century. Such at least is the opinion of H. E. Korth, who has pointed to remarkable similarities between the lives and careers of the Frankish princes of the sixth century and those of the mid- to late seventh.[1]

Having said that, we cannot fail to be struck by the parallels between the historical situation in the Frankish lands during the mid-seventh and mid-tenth centuries. We note in particular the establishment of an indepen-

---

1 See E. H. Korth, "Twins in the 'Pippin-Erae'" at www.jahr1000wen.de

dent and predominantly German-speaking kingdom in the east during both centuries.

Bearing all this in mind, I would suggest that Henry the Fowler flourished early in the seventh century and that he was a contemporary and adversary of the Merovingian kings Clothair II and Dagobert I.

SPAIN IN THE SEVENTH AND TENTH CENTURIES

When we come to consider Spain, the need for a drastic rewrite of Islam's early history, which we considered in the preceding chapter, becomes all too apparent.

According to the textbooks, Spain was conquered by the Arabs in 711 — almost eighty years after they are said to have emerged from Arabia and began the subjugation of the Near East. However, apart from a pitifully few finds of doubtful provenance, the earliest archaeological trace of Islam in the Iberian Peninsula comes in the first half of the tenth century. These finds are generally associated with Abd' er Rahman III (reign commencing in 912). This man was a well-known warrior and conqueror who launched numerous expeditions against the still-surviving Christian strongholds in the north of the country. Abd' er Rahman III was succeeded by Al-Mansur, another conqueror, who plundered the shrine of Santiago de Compostela and launched raids across the Pyrenees, replicating in many ways the deeds attributed to the conqueror Musa in the early eighth century. And indeed everything we read about Spain in the tenth and early eleventh centuries looks like a carbon-copy rerun of everything that happened in the eighth century. Abd' er Rahman III's life and career for example looks strikingly similar to that of his namesake and supposed ancestor Abd' er Rahman I, who, in the middle of the eighth century founded the Spanish Emirate and completed the conquest of the peninsula, striking against the Christian princes still holding out in the north of the country. In Illig's words:

"It is just in the 10th century that we find the struggle between Christians and Muslims raging throughout the land. A stronghold like Toledo was conquered and lost more than once. Abd er-Rahman III is the most notable character. During his reign (916–961) for the first time, the dominion of the Omayyads was secured (renewed?). As the title of Caliph indicated, he united in himself both temporal and spiritual authority. His possessions in Spain consisted of much more than Andalusia. His defeat at the Battle of Simancas in 939, best demonstrates the extent of his influence. Simancas lay between Salamanca and Valladolid on the Duoro, marking therefore the most northerly position of the Arab troops. In spite of this defeat, the Omayyad

State reaches its apogee in the middle of the 10th century. Reflecting this is the fact that the Christian king of Leon could only hold the throne with Omayyad help. In 980 there emerged once again in Al-Mansur a conqueror in the grand style. He burned Leon, Barcelona and Santiago de Compostela, and advanced even over the Pyrenees. His progress was only halted with his death in the year 1002."[1]

So, whilst supposedly almost the whole of Spain had been conquered in the early eighth century, we find that in the middle of the tenth century the process of Islamic conquest was still under way, with Abd' er Rahman III stopped at the Battle of Simancas, in the middle of the country. Only later, in the time of Al-Mansur, do the conquerors reach the Pyrenees and beyond. Thus it would appear that both Abd' er Rahman I and Abd' er Rahman III lived during the Islamic conquest of Iberia. And there are other parallels. Both Abd' er Rahman I and Abd' er Rahman III are said to have done important work in the Great Mosque of Cordoba, gradually changing its outline and design from the earlier cathedral of Saint Vincent. There is, however, one great difference between the two Abd' er Rahmans: whilst the one of the eighth century has left virtually no archaeological trace of his existence, his supposed ancestor of the tenth century has left abundant proof of his life.

Now if Illig is correct and events of the tenth century need to be back-dated into the seventh, this would mean that Abd' er Rahman III flourished in the seventh century and not (like his apparent alter-ego Abd' er Rahman I) in the eighth. In short, the Islamic conquest of Spain must have occurred at least several decades before the date given in the textbooks. And this in turn would suggest that Islam spread through North Africa — on its way to Spain — a good deal earlier than is imagined. In short, Islam must have appeared in the world stage many years — quite possibly up to half a century — before the history books allow.

All this of course is in accordance with what we found in the previous chapter, where we learned that the early history of Islam, as it is now understood, is a complete fiction, and that a prototype Islam — the "Christian" Ebionite cult — existed and flourished throughout Arabia centuries before the supposed life of Muhammad. We saw too that the war which the Persian King Chosroes II (who had converted to some form of Christianity) launched against the Byzantines in 602 bore all the hallmarks of a religiously-inspired crusade or jihad. The evidence further suggested that the Christianity adopted by Chosroes II was the Arabian version. In short, the Persians were allies

---

1 Illig, *Wer hat and der Uhr gedreht?* pp. 104-5

of the Arabs, and it was the "Islamicized" Persians who conducted the great conquests in the Middle East and North Africa which were later attributed to a few Arab nomads on camels. This being the case, the Islamic conquest of Egypt is identical to the Persian conquest of that country, and must be dated around 620 rather than 640. It must have been Persian armies too that overthrew the mighty Byzantine defensive works in Cyrenicaea, though the conquest of Carthage and the rest of North Africa would have been carried out after the Arabs under Mu'awiya had seized control of the Sassanid government. Nonetheless, the whole progress of Islamic conquest across North Africa must have been much quicker than the textbooks allow, and we may guess that Muslim armies stood ready to attack Spain by the middle of the seventh century.

If all of this is correct, the entire narrative of the Islamic invasion of Spain needs to be re-examined in a fundamental way, and we need to forget the idea of a sweeping and devastating Muslim onslaught overwhelming the entire Peninsula in a couple of years. If the Invasion commenced in the middle of the seventh century, it would appear to have taken the Islamic forces several decades to push northwards towards the Pyrenees. This latter is suggested, as we saw above, by the fact that Abd' er Rahman III, in the middle of the tenth century (which is identical to the mid-seventh century), was still encountering fierce resistance in the north of Spain in his time.

But aside from pointing to the mid-seventh century, is it possible to be more precise with regard to the Islamic Conquest?

In fact, several pieces of evidence combine to suggest that the Invasion commenced during or near the reign of the Visigothic king Recceswinth (generally dated 653–672).

In this regard it is worth noting that some features of late Visigothic architecture, from the time of Recceswinth onwards, are very reminiscent of early Iberian Romanesque of the late tenth and eleventh centuries. This is particularly so with regard to the use of cut-stone in churches and other public buildings, a feature only encountered again in of the eleventh century (eighth century in Illig's scheme). Furthermore, some unique features of late seventh century Visigothic architecture — in particular the famous horseshoe arch — look suspiciously as if they were inspired by Islamic ideas. Recceswinth himself, who left a fine church featuring one of the first examples of a horseshoe arch, also left several brilliant votive crowns which were uncovered amongst the treasure of Guarrazar in the nineteenth century. Historians accept that these jewels were almost certainly buried for safekeeping during the Muslim Conquest.

Whilst crowns belonging to kings earlier than Recceswinth were also found at Guarrazar, none belonging to later rulers were discovered, which suggests that the hoard was buried in the lifetime of Recceswinth or shortly thereafter.

During the reign of Recceswinth's father Khindaswinth a Germanic-named official of the Byzantines, Ardabast, fled to the Gothic court in Spain, where he married a niece of the king. This must have occurred around 645. Strangely, another Ardabast, supposedly a descendant of the first, became an important ally and collaborator of the Muslims after their conquest, receiving from them several royal estates of the Hispano-Gothic house.[1]

I would suggest that the Ardabast who collaborated with the Muslims was one and the same as the Ardabast who fled from Constantinople around 645.

The Islamic Conquest, as it is now understood, seems strangely disjointed, with Tariq the Berber, accompanied by a numerically tiny force, sweeping through much of the country in less than two years beginning in 711. So successful is this early Muslim onslaught that Islamic armies were supposedly crossing the Pyrenees from 715 and striking deep into France in the years following — before being finally stopped by Charles Martel in the middle of Gaul in 732. Yet for all their early successes we hear that Abd' er Rahman I had to overcome fierce resistance in the north of Spain in the middle of the eighth century.

Bearing all this in mind, I would suggest that Tariq's initial invasion occurred around 650 and did not penetrate much beyond the south of the country. Musa may have reached further north, but did not succeed in eliminating the Christian rulers of the north, or even of the center around Toledo. It was left to Abd' er Rahman I (and III) to complete the conquest of the entire land around the 660s. One of his opponents was almost certainly Recceswinth, who seems to have been an alter-ego of Abd' er Rahman III's opponent Ramiro II of Leon. Historians are agreed that the kings of Asturias and Leon in the late ninth and tenth centuries actively sought to "recreate" the Visigothic monarchy.[2]

That the clash with Islam came in the seventh and not the eighth century is also suggested by the increasingly anti-Jewish measures enacted at the various Councils of Toledo (beginning with the Fourth Council in 633). It is

1 Harold V. Livermore, *The Origins of Spain and Portugal* (George Allen and Unwin, Ltd., London, 1971), p. 211
2 Ibid., p. 388. "The greatest ruler of the Asturian monarchy, Alfonso III [866–911], had a clear vision of a restoration of the Gothic monarchy throughout Spain ..." Ibid.

recognized that the anti-Jewish pronouncements of Toledo were prompted by fear of an impending conflict with the Muslims.[1] The problem here, of course, is that the Jews would scarcely have been seen as a threat in 633, when the Fourth Council introduced stringent measures against them, if accepted chronology is correct. If on the other hand Islamic rule had already spread over North Africa by 633, then the pronouncements of the Fourth Council begin to make some sense.

Yet even allowing for this adjustment the situation is problematic. We are told that Iberian Jews assisted the Muslims in their conquest of Spain — a claim that seems barely credible if Muhammad had carried out the massacres of Jews accredited to him in Arabia in the early seventh century. The Jews were at that time, as always, an international community with very good lines of communication over wide areas. Had a man called Muhammad really carried out massacres of Jews in Arabia around the 610s and 620s, they would have been acutely aware of the dangers to themselves of an Islamic conquest of Spain and would scarcely have co-operated with incoming Muslim forces. However, if Islam as we know it did not then exist, if only an Ebionite or Arab Christian proto-Islam without yet a Qur'an or Hadith, was then extant, then Jewish co-operation with the invaders might begin to make sense. We know that the Jews of Syria — as well as numerous Arab allies — co-operated with the Persians during their invasion of that territory in 614 and they are said to have participated in the massacre of the Christian population of Jerusalem carried out by the Persians in the latter year.

BYZANTIUM IN THE SEVENTH AND TENTH CENTURIES

When we look at the world of Byzantium and how its seventh and tenth century histories can be knitted together following the removal of the phantom time, our attention is immediately drawn to the life and career of Heraclius. It was, as we saw, in the latter's reign that the Eastern Empire first came into armed conflict with the Arabs, a disastrous encounter which resulted in the loss of almost all the empire's Asiatic and North African territories. Illig has suggested that the reign of Heraclius was much shorter than is generally allowed, and that, after the ignominious loss of Jerusalem and the Holy Land, he was probably killed in action around 620. The victorious armies of Chosroes II, along with numerous Arab allies, then prolonged their march of conquest to Libya and westwards to Carthage.

The Byzantine historians of course tell a different story. They hold that, after suffering a series of military catastrophes, culminating in the loss of

---

1 Ibid., pp. 205-265

almost all the empire's Asiatic possessions and the appearance of a Persian army near the walls of Constantinople, Heraclius turned the tide in a most spectacular way: He is said to have led an army of picked men, just five thousand strong, into the heart of the Persian Empire (going as far as Isfahan), inflicting at the same time a series of crushing defeats on the Sassanids, and extracting from them a humiliating armistice. The Persians, we are told, were compelled to evacuate all the territories they had conquered in North Africa and Syria and furthermore to return to the Byzantines the sacred relics — including the Holy Cross — they had earlier looted from Jerusalem. The Persian sources, however (as we have seen), have no record of these events and on the contrary speak of Chosroes II as "the undefeatable."

The Byzantine records tell how in his latter years Heraclius suffered a further series of military catastrophes, this time at the hands of the Arabs, losing to these invaders all the territories he had previously lost and reconquered from the Persians.

As we saw in Chapter 4, none of this narrative makes much sense or corresponds with the discoveries of archeology. Nor does it make sense from a historical or military perspective. The astonishing counter-offensive which Heraclius is said to have launched against the Persians and which saw him march into the heart of Iran with a mere 5,000 men is quite simply beyond belief. Even the mighty Alexander of Macedon needed an army of 30,000 to conquer Persia — and Heraclius was by no means a military genius in Alexander's mold. And the strangeness of Heraclius' story has long struck historians. In the words of Gibbon: "Of the characters conspicuous in history, that of Heraclius is one of the most extraordinary and inconsistent. In the first and last years of a long reign, the emperor appears to be the slave of sloth, of pleasure, or of superstition, the careless and impotent spectator of the public calamities. But the languid mists of the morning and evening are separated by the brightness of the meridian sun: the Arcadius of the palace, arose the Caesar of the camp; and the honor of Rome and Heraclius was gloriously retrieved by the exploits and trophies of six adventurous campaigns" (Chapter 46). Gibbon goes on to lament that it was the duty of the Byzantine historians to explain these extraordinary inconsistencies and turnarounds, a duty they failed to fulfill.

The evidence, as we have seen, is that these latter expeditions of Heraclius are pure fiction. Yet if that be the case, what, we might ask, was the purpose of such an invention? The Arabs usurped the Sassanid throne and rewrote history to disguise the fact and justify their actions: But what was the motive of the Byzantines? The answer, I believe, is fairly straightforward:

in an intensely religious age the loss of the sacred relics at Jerusalem in 614 was a moral catastrophe. At some stage, probably a century or more later, a new set of sacred relics, used to bolster the faith of the populace in their desperate struggle with the Arabs, appeared in Constantinople. These were without question fakes; yet it was important for the people to believe they were genuine: hence it was important to create a narrative of how they came to be back in the possession of the empire. That narrative was Heraclius' victorious wars against the Persians in the middle of his reign.

Concocting a history in which Heraclius turned the tide of war against the Persians, and then lost everything a second time to the Arabs, meant giving him a reign much longer than he really enjoyed. Thus 641 was fixed as the year of his death.

Everything then suggests that Heraclius died shortly after the Persian conquest of Syria and Egypt, around 620, and that immediately afterward the empire went into precipitate decline. Very few, if any, major buildings or material finds can be attributed to the emperors who are said to have followed Heraclius. A few coins, usually of silver or bronze, can be securely tied to Constans II, who is said to have succeeded Heraclius after the extremely brief reign (no more than a few months) of Constantine III and Heracleon. A small handful of coins attributable to several other emperors, usually of poor quality (often of an emperor named Leo), then occur before the appearance of the well-recognized mints of Constantine VII/Porphyrogenitus, in the early tenth century — a full three centuries later. Since we know that Constantine VII reigned until 959 (i.e., 659 or rather 662 according to Illig), this means that all the emperors between Heraclius and him — there are said to have been twenty-five — must be placed in the few intervening years. However, because Heraclius is said to have reigned until 641 and Constantine VII is credited with a forty-eight year reign (beginning in 911, i.e., Illig's 614), it is clear that neither of these monarchs can have reigned anywhere near as long as they are credited, and that furthermore almost all the emperors placed between them are fictitious. Indeed, since only two of these, Constans II and Leo (III or VI) have any archeology at all, we can conclude that they are the only two genuine historical figures between Heraclius and Constantine VII. The Emperor Leo can only have been Leo "the Isaurian," who launched the Iconoclasm episode, supposedly in the middle of the eighth century. Iconoclasm, it is well understood, was an extreme reaction to the existential crisis facing the empire following the terrible losses to the Arabs in the seventh century. That it really occurred is beyond question; almost all pictorial representations of Christ and the saints predating the seventh century have disappeared from the Byzantine world. The episode of destruction is generally placed in the eighth century, right in the middle of the Dark Age, so that here we have a prime example of a real event which has been placed chronologically in an epoch that never existed.

Where then does all this leave us?

Well, for one thing, it means that after the ephemeral reigns of Constantine III and Heracleon, Constans II sat the throne, for a handful of years at least. His reign cannot have been long. We know that during his time Constantinople itself was threatened by the Arabs under the Umayyad Caliph Mu'awiya), who laid siege to the city for four years — supposedly 674–8, but far more probably around 645. The terrible crisis facing Byzantium then led to iconoclasm under the next emperor, who was named Leo. His reign too cannot have been of great length, and we may be justified in placing the accession of Constantine VII around 650. With the latter we emerge again into the light of real history.

Fig. 6. The Reconstructed History of the Seventh Century

DATE	FRANCE AND GERMANY	SPAIN	BYZANTIUM	PERSIA AND MIDDLE EAST
735	Conrad II	Rodrigo of Vivar (El Cid) campaigns against Muslims.	Michael IV	
				Tugrul Beg begins the conquest of Anatolia.
715	Henry II	Don Pelayo. Beginning of Reconquista	Constantine VIII	Seljuk Turks rule Persia and Mesopotamia.
	Otto III establishes Anno Domini calendar.		John I	Al-Mu'tamid
695		Al-Mansur destroys Compostela and crosses the Pyrenees		Al-Mu'tasim. Capital moved to Samarra.

	Otto II			Harun al-Rashid. Great age of Baghdad.
675			Basil II	Al-Mansur. Building of Baghdad.
	Otto I. Victory over the Magyars. Revival of Western Empire.	Abd' er Rahman I/III	Romanus I	Al-Saffah. Establishment of Abassid Dynasty.
655	Victory of Henry the Fowler over Avars/Magyars	Recceswinth/ Ramiro II Islamic Invasion	Constantine VII	Abd al-Malik. Arabization of Ummayad court.
	Henry the Fowler establishes an independent state east of the Rhine. Beginning of the Viking Wars.	Khindaswinth	Leo III and Iconoclasm	Mu'awiya establishes Arab rule over Persian Empire.
635	Dagobert I (division of Merovingian state). Beginning of obscure period of Merovingian history.	Sisenand		Yazdegerd III involved in war with Arab mercenaries, leading to Arab coup d'etat.
	Death of Clothair II (629)	Swinthila	Constans II (Constantinople besieged by Persians/Arabs).	Death of Chosroes II (628)
615		Sisebut	Heraclius (war with Persia, and loss of African and Asian provinces).	War with Byzantium. (Persia, with Arab allies, conquers Syria)
	Clothair II (unified Merovingian state).			Chosroes II converts to Ebionite (proto-Islamic) faith. Circa 590.

CHAPTER 6: A STRANGE NEW WORLD

Accepting that Illig is correct has dramatic consequences for almost every area of history. Most obviously, if the years between 614 and 911 (or 914) did not exist, this means that all dates post-911 must be reduced by almost three centuries. Thus for example the Norman Conquest of England did not occur in 1066 but in 766, or, more precisely, 769, if Illig's chronology is to be followed exactly. In the same way, the First Crusade would not have been launched in 1095, but in 795 or shortly thereafter. The widespread feeling among historians therefore that the Crusades represented the Christian response to the Islamic conquests is therefore stunningly confirmed. Remove the three hundred years of the Dark Age and the Crusades, at last, make perfect sense.

No area of European history can escape the consequences of such an upheaval in the chronological order, but what strikes one most, from the new perspective, is the speed of historical developments as they occurred in real time. Processes which we had previously imagined took many centuries are now revealed to have occurred in a few decades. We are struck too by the medieval world's proximity to the Roman one. The Norman Invasion of England did not occur eleven centuries after Caesar but only eight, and the strikingly Roman-looking feel of so much of early medieval culture begins to make perfect sense. The late Roman art and architecture of the Merovingians and Visigoths, which survived and flourished into the seventh century now appears — rightly — as the immediate predecessor and ancestor of the Roman-style "Romanesque" art and architecture of Germany, France and Spain of the tenth and eleventh centuries.

Everywhere we see a picture of continuity rather than fracture. The survival of Latin as the language of learning and the church is but one facet of the all-pervasive Romanness that now emerges; and we can at last agree with the revisionists who in recent decades have spoken insistently of the "Vanishing Paradigm of the Fall of Rome." Truly, as they say, Rome, or at least Roman civilization, did not fall, but merely developed into medieval civilization. Thus the great "rebirth" of European civilization which occurred in the late tenth and early eleventh centuries, and which saw the resumption of construction of massive monumental architecture and the building of new towns, actually occurred in the late seventh and early eighth centuries and formed a continuum with the rebirth and revival of Europe which had commenced so promisingly in the sixth century. Taken out of its proper context, the tenth/eleventh century "Renaissance" makes no sense at all, and historians struggle to explain it. That it was accompanied by a massive increase in population and a general expansion of agriculture is evident to all. Why this increase and expansion should have occurred in the tenth and eleventh centuries has, however, hitherto been mysterious. In the words of Hugh Trevor-Roper, the change that came over Europe was great, though "Exactly what that ... was we can hardly say."[1] Nonetheless, "one element in the chemical change of the eleventh century was undoubtedly a great, though to us unmeasurable, increase in population, and one cause, or at least concomitant, of this increase of population was a series of technical improvements which increased the productivity of the land."[2] He then goes on to suggest that the adoption of the moldboard plow was a development of the tenth or eleventh century, and that this new technology facilitated a great expansion of agriculture. The problem with this explanation, of course, is that the moldboard plow was known since the fourth century and had become common in temperate Europe by the sixth. Why then did it fail to produce an expanded population until the eleventh century?

But if the "Renaissance" of the tenth and eleventh centuries actually occurred in the seventh and eighth, then the expansion of populations and towns makes perfect sense and is part of a normal organic development that had commenced in the sixth century. And it is clear too what prompted this revival: The adoption of Christianity, which we mentioned in Chapter 1, had everywhere the same result: an immediate and fairly dramatic increase in

1 Trevor-Roper, op cit., p. 113
2 Ibid., pp. 113-4

the population. During the second and third centuries this was felt most in the eastern territories of the Roman Empire, where Christianity (and Judaism) was strongest. Indeed by the fifth and sixth centuries Christianity had so transformed the Levantine world that cities and towns were more populous and numerous than ever, and historians speak of a "Golden Age" of Late Classical civilization in the region. The west, being further from the core areas of Christianity, was converted later. Yet here too the moment of conversion marks a new epoch of growth and expansion. Spain, with her enormous Jewish population, was among the first of the western provinces to become Christian (most early converts to Christianity were from among the Jews), and Spain was likewise earliest to show signs of revival and expansion. Uniquely in the west, and for the first time since the early Caesars, by the sixth century the kings of Spain began to erect entirely new cities. Gaul was converted somewhat later than Spain, but here too, around the first quarter of the seventh century, archaeologists noted the first signs of expanding towns and populations. Germany too was converted at the same time, and the great medieval towns of that country began to spring up everywhere.

Ireland had been converted a good deal earlier, in the fifth century, and here too there appeared all the signs of expansion and growth. As well as adopting Roman civilization wholesale — including study of the Latin language and the imitation of Roman architecture — the Irish now began sending out colonies to various parts of the British Isles, some of which became thoroughly Hibernicized. How else to explain the adoption of the Gaelic language in Scotland — even though the Irish failed to conquer the country?[1]

The massive expansion of Christianity into northern and eastern Europe, which historians have hitherto ascribed to the late tenth and eleventh centuries, can now be seen as part of the organic growth of Christianity which began in Gaul and Germany during the fifth and sixth centuries. Thus Poland, Hungary, Scandinavia and Russia must really have been converted — and added to Latin civilization — in the late seventh and early eighth centuries; which means that by 700 or 720 at latest the borders of Christendom and Roman civilization stood at the Urals in the east and the Arctic Circle in the north. Christian missionaries and monks had therefore achieved in a few decades what the legions of Rome had failed to achieve in many centuries.

Such a fact will have profound implications for our understanding of Christianity and its impact upon history.

---

1 The language of the native Caledonians was presumably fairly close to the Celtic dialect of Ireland, yet by the sixth century the two were sufficiently different to warrant the services of interpreters, if we are to believe contemporary accounts.

With this expansion came a veritable tidal wave of new technologies and learning. Most of the new ideas, many of which were of epoch-making importance, arrived from the east — usually from China or India. And again, this was a process which began in the sixth century (with the arrival of the stirrup and silk-making), then was mysteriously interrupted for three centuries only to recommence (equally mysteriously) in the tenth century. These new ideas created a civilization that was far more technically advanced than Rome had ever been. Nonetheless, it was a civilization that often lacked the efficiency and even the rationality of Rome. The musings of an Isidore of Seville (seventh century) on etymology and natural history sound puerile and ignorant when compared with the writings of a Pliny. And yet this newly Christianized and Latinized Europe was far from being barbarous: elaborate churches, castles and palaces were springing up everywhere from the Atlantic to the Urals, and monastic institutions were propagating the learning of Greece and Rome, in both Greek and Latin, all over the continent.

Many of the new technologies which entered Europe at this time came by way of the newly Islamicized Near East. These must have arrived, as common sense indicates, in the seventh century and not the tenth, as history, with its "Dark Age" has hitherto insisted. This means that the Arab blockade of the Mediterranean, which Henri Pirenne blamed for precipitating the "Dark Age" in Europe, did not entirely sever all commercial and cultural contact along the trade-routes of the "Middle Sea." Does this then mean that the Arabs were a beneficial force in the Mediterranean and that Pirenne got it wrong? This is an important question that requires careful consideration.

Europe and the East

Irrespective of how we view Islam and its impact upon Western civilization, it is surely no coincidence that the confused epoch we now call the "Dark Age" coincided precisely with the appearance of the Muslim faith on the world stage. What emerges very clearly from Illig's redating of the early Middle Ages is that the appearance of Islam marked the definitive end of Late Antiquity and the commencement of the medieval age. The very confusion which allowed the phantom centuries to be implanted into the calendar and the Dark Age myth to be created in the first place was a direct result of momentous events happening in the eastern Mediterranean in the first half of the seventh century.

We know that immediately prior to the great war with Persia which commenced in 602, the Byzantine lands of Anatolia, Syria and Egypt were enjoying a period of unprecedented prosperity. We have seen how archaeologists describe this epoch as a "Golden Age" in the eastern Mediterranean. Cities flourished as never before and great centers of learning, in Alexandria, Heliopolis, Antioch, Ephesus and elsewhere, preserved and added to the knowledge of the Greeks and Romans. Within a very short time of the Persian and Arab conquests these centers were mostly defunct and many of the great cities of the area were in terminal decline. Perhaps within fifty years of the Arab conquests huge swathes of territory in the Middle East and North Africa, which had until then supported a thriving agriculture and prosperous cities, was turned into a semi-inhabited wasteland. By the middle of the eighth century the population of the Middle East and North Africa had registered a decline estimated at anything between threefold and tenfold. The "revived" urban environments which archaeologists regard as having appeared in the tenth century (just as in Europe) are usually quite small in comparison with the Byzantine cities of the sixth century which they replaced.

How is this to be explained?

The topic of Islam's impact upon Mediterranean civilization is one that has generated heated debate over the past century, a debate that has become arguably even more heated in the wake of the 9/11 atrocities and the revival of an aggressive and expansionist Islam over the past few decades. Suffice to note here that the best evidence suggests that the arrival in the Byzantine territories of Syria and North Africa of nomad Arabs with their herds of goats devastated the complex system of irrigation and terracing which the Romans had maintained for centuries.[1] Yet that in itself is insufficient to explain the destruction of the entire economy of the region. Native husbandmen, we might imagine, would have taken exception to Arab newcomers grazing their goats and camels in their cornfields. This would certainly have occurred at the beginning; but the provisions of Islamic law, as enshrined in the *sharia* code, would ensure that such objections would soon be silenced. Under the provisions of *sharia* law, unbelievers do not share equal rights with Muslims. In any dispute there is a tendency for the Muslim appellant to claim the infidel has insulted Islam or Muhammad. This is a capital offense in Islam, and since the testimony of a Muslim always trumps that of an infidel, the latter was (and in some areas still is) invariably arrested and put to death. Under such circumstances it is perfectly understandable that

---

1 See e.g., Rhoads Murphey, "The Decline of North Africa since the Roman Occupation: Climatic or Human?" *ANNALS, Association of American Geographers*, Vol. XLI, no. 2, (June, 1951).

Christian or Jewish farmers in the Middle East and North Africa would learn not to complain if they saw Arab nomads grazing their herds in their fields.

In such circumstances large areas of previously irrigated and cultivated land might soon be reduced to wasteland; and it has to be admitted that this is precisely what we observe throughout the conquered territories in the seventh century.

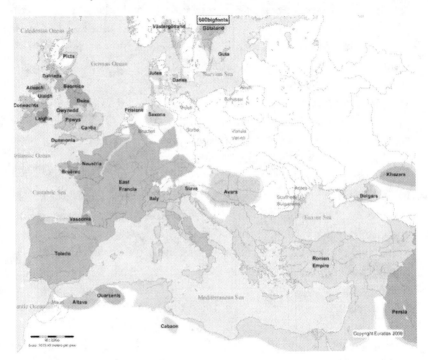

Fig. 7 A. Map of Europe, circa AD 600.

The impact of Islam on Europe was more nuanced, but it was also dramatic. Pirenne had stressed that the Muslims broke the unity of the old classical civilization by blockading the Mediterranean. Cut off from the higher centers of culture in the east, Europe was left to its own devices, and the focus of cultural and economic activity moved north, towards northern Gaul, Germany, Britain and Scandinavia.

There is no question that Pirenne was largely right in this regard, notwithstanding attempts of mainstream scholars to debunk him over the decades. Critics have stressed that trade — albeit mainly in slaves — did continue in the Mediterranean after the appearance of Islam, and they have pointed to the influx into Europe of new technologies from the tenth century onwards (which of course is Illig's seventh century).

On the first of these objections, it has to be conceded that trade in slaves can hardly be considered normal economic activity. The slaves the Muslims desired were white-skinned Europeans, and these were obtained either by raiding towns and villages throughout southern Europe, or by purchasing them from Viking freebooters. And indeed it is now widely understood that the entire Viking phenomenon was called forth by the Islamic world's demand for European slaves. The slaves sold to the Caliphate by the Vikings were often from eastern Europe — and our very word "slave" is derived from "Slav." At this stage most of the Slavs were still pagans. But the Vikings, as everyone knows, also preyed upon Christian Europeans in Britain, France and Germany. Many of these too made their way into the harems of the caliphs and emirs.

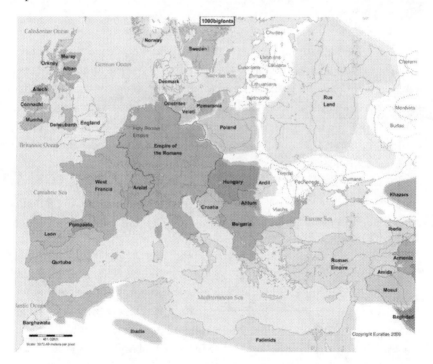

Fig. 7 B. Map of Europe, circa 1000 (actually 700, in Illig's chronology). This illustrates the dramatic expansion of Christendom in the century between 600 and 700, if Illig is correct.

It can be no coincidence that it was just in the first few decades of the seventh century that the previous pattern of settlement in southern Europe, with scattered and undefended lowland villas, was replaced by a retreat to defended hilltop redoubts — the first medieval castles.

The slave trade therefore is associated with piracy, and piracy, if it is endemic, means the end of most if not all normal trade. And the fact that normal trade did cease is proved beyond question by the disappearance from Europe, from the middle of the seventh century, of certain products which had previously been imported into the west in great quantities. Pirenne mentioned several of these, such as spices, wines, silk, papyrus, etc. He might also have noted the disappearance of good-quality soda for glass production, which meant the termination of the burgeoning Merovingian glass industry in the seventh century.

Yet, as mentioned above, Pirenne's critics have also pointed to the influx of eastern technologies and ideas into the west in the tenth (and actually in Illig's scheme the seventh) century. If this is the case, how can there have been a blockade, as Pirenne claimed?

As answer to this, it is sufficient to note that a new idea or technology may be transmitted from one civilization to another by a single knowledgeable individual and does not need the assistance of regular trading relations. It is known for a fact that several of the new ideas, such as the Arabic numeral system (which was actually Indian) reached Europe through a mere handful of Jewish refugees, who arrived in France and Germany from North Africa and Spain in the late tenth century (actually late seventh) to escape persecution. In addition, a small number of Europeans — often in disguise — crossed the borders of the Islamic world in search of knowledge. It seems that Gerbert of Aurillac, the genius of the tenth (seventh) century, may have been one of these.

At this point the reader might note that since the Arabs possessed knowledge and technologies the Europeans desired, this at least proves that they cannot have been as obscurantist and anti-science as is commonly imagined. Again, however, Illig's thesis casts a whole new light on this. When Islam conquered the Middle East and North Africa, it took control of the major centers of classical civilization. In Anatolia, Mesopotamia, Syria, Egypt and North Africa there existed vast and wealthy cities beside which the "cities" of Europe looked like mere villages. Even at the height of the Roman Empire, under the Caesars, Europe was an economic and cultural backwater. Aside from Rome herself, Europe had no real urban centers. With the relocation to Byzantium in the fourth century the economic stagnation of the West only increased. Christianity, it is true, by encouraging a higher birth rate, did provide a stimulus which eventually led to a powerful and vibrant Europe; but the Christianization of Europe had barely begun by the sixth century.

So, in taking control of the prosperous and advanced lands of the Middle East and North Africa, Islam gained possession of all the important centers of civilization and wealth in the seventh century. Pre-Islamic Sassanid Persia was already, by the sixth century, a conduit for the importation of new technologies and ideas from China and India into the occident. This continued for a short time after the Islamicization of Iran; but it seems to have been a very short time. The weight of Islamic theocracy was soon to put paid to most economic and scholarly innovation. We know that by the middle of the eleventh (i.e., eighth) century the Islamic world had begun to lose its advantage, and that from then on Europe became able to compete. This means, in Illig's scheme, that by the middle of the eighth century — say around 750 — the Islamic world had already squandered the gigantic head-start it had inherited from the Sassanids and conquered Byzantines just a hundred years earlier.

Indeed, by the middle of the eighth century Europe was ready to counterattack.

And this of course brings us to the whole question of the Crusades. Everything about the latter series of wars, which commenced officially in 1096 but which had really begun in Spain and Sicily in the 1030s, would suggest that they represented a European response to the Islamic wars of conquest. However, since these latter are supposed to have begun about four centuries earlier, it has been customary not to see the Crusades as a response to them. Instead, the Crusades are widely held to be an almost incomprehensible outburst of European aggression (a kind of early proto-colonialism) against a quiescent and peaceful Islamic world.

Applying Illig's new chronology, the Crusades finally make sense: The march of conquest of the Seljuk Turks through Anatolia to the gates of Constantinople, which precipitated the First Crusade, is now seen as an event of the eighth century, and the final great wave of Islamic conquest which had begun just a century earlier.

APPENDIX: THE ASTRONOMICAL EVIDENCE

Illig's thesis rests primarily upon the evidence of archeology, and this evidence is fairly conclusive. Yet I would be remiss if I concluded without mentioning the fact that his thesis also has very powerful astronomical, or rather calendrical, support. This concerns the Gregorian Calendar and the circumstances surrounding its introduction in 1582. The latter was intended to replace the old Julian Calendar, introduced by Julius Caesar in 45 B.C., a necessary reform owing to the inaccuracy of the Julian system. The Julian Calendar treated the year as exactly 365.25 days long — an extra day was added every fourth year, or Leap Year. But the year is not exactly 365.25 days; it is more precisely 365.2422 days, which means that, following the Julian system, about eleven minutes are added every year; and this, in the 1,627 years that had apparently elapsed between Caesar's reform and Pope Gregory's, should have produced an error of roughly thirteen days. In fact, the astronomers and mathematicians working for the Pope found that the civil calendar needed to be adjusted by only ten days, and it thus appears that the calendar counted roughly three centuries which never existed.

The normal explanation for this discrepancy is the claim that the Julian calendar must have originally marked the solstices and equinoxes at a different time from us. Thus for example it is claimed that Caesar had March 25 as the spring equinox, and that this date was used until the Council of Nicea in A.D. 325 (or some other time in the third or fourth century), when the calendar was "updated" and the equinoxes recalibrated according to contemporary observations. In other words, by the time of the Nicean Council the spring equinox would, owing to the error inbuilt in the Julian Calendar, have drifted to March 21, and the Church

Fathers, employing new observations, would have used that date to mark the equinox.

Gregory's astronomers therefore had only to correct the error which accumulated in the centuries between the Council of Nicea and 1528, which of course is a span of 1,257 years. Ten days is therefore the correct margin of error.

Illig has countered this by pointing out that a movement of the equinoxes away from their proper positions is extremely difficult to detect without sophisticated mathematical equipment, and it is therefore unlikely that the Church Fathers at Nicea would have been aware that there was anything wrong with the calendar. Even in Pope Gregory's time, when the civil calendar had drifted ten days away from the astronomical, there was much debate as to what might be the reason. It took some of the greatest minds of the time (the Renaissance) to figure out that the problem was the Julian Calendar itself. Furthermore, by the time of the Nicean Council the drift of the calendar would have produced a spring equinox in March 22 or even 23, not March 21, which again makes it seem likely that in using March 21 as the date the Church Fathers were simply following long-established custom.

In addition to all this, Illig has now produced fairly definitive documentary proof that the Romans from Caesar onwards did indeed celebrate the spring equinox on March 21. Illig was informed of the relevant document, Columella's *De Re Rustica*, by W. X. Frank, in 2011.[1] In the latter work Columella refers to Virgil, who remarked that the sowing of wheat should only be done when the Pleiades have set. He adds,

> Now they are "hidden" on the thirty-second day after the autumnal equinox, which usually falls on the ninth day before the Calends of October [i.e., the 23rd of September].

Since an autumn equinox on September 23 gives a spring equinox on March 21, it is certain that in Virgil's time, around A.D. 60, the spring equinox was on March 21. In short, from at least A.D. 60 onwards the spring equinox was marked on the same day as on the Gregorian Calendar, and at the very least Gregory's astronomers should have had to take thirteen days from the calendar to rectify the mistake. That they had to remove only ten days means that 1,522 years cannot have elapsed between Virgil and Gregory. The true span of time separating them must have been roughly 300 years short of 1,522 years.

1 Illig, "Calendar Reforms of Caesar and Gregory XIII," *Society for Interdisciplinary Studies: Chronology and Catastrophism Review*, (2001), pp. 3-6

* * *

On the subject of calendars, the reader might well ask whether eclipses might be brought to bear on the subject of chronology. These, after all, can be "retrocalculated" from our own time into antiquity. The works of the ancient authors frequently mention solar eclipses and often provide the precise location from which they were visible. This is important, since an eclipse of the sun, whilst a spectacular event, is only visible over a comparatively narrow strip of the earth's surface.

As might be imagined, Illig's critics were in fact very quick to use the evidence of eclipses against him. The great majority of these, being non-specialists, imagined that the record of solar eclipses, as found in the ancient writers, matches the actual eclipses as calculated by modern astronomers. Yet, as Illig replied, the evidence of eclipses most certainly does not support conventional chronology. Almost without exception, the astronomically calculated eclipses occur at a different time to that recorded in the ancient writings. In the one or two cases where experts claim agreement between the two, the precise location of the eclipse is not given.

Take for example the eclipse that is said to have occurred at the time of Jesus' death — presumably around the year A.D. 33. In fact, astronomers have to concede that no eclipse would have been visible in Jerusalem at that time. An eclipse would have been visible in A.D. 29, but that would have occurred in November, whereas Jesus died in the springtime, either in March or April (feast of the Passover). An eclipse would have been visible on April 30, A.D. 59, but this is far outside the lifetime of Jesus. (Scholars concede that the life of Jesus is not accurately aligned to secular history, and his precise birth date, for example, is still disputed — though it is generally placed between about 6 and 4 B.C.)

The "eclipse" of Jesus' death then is not an event that can be used to support conventional chronology. It has to be conceded, of course, that the Gospels do not specifically refer to eclipse — simply to a "darkness" which came over the earth between the sixth and the ninth hour. This last detail certainly does not sound like an eclipse, since these last only a few minutes. Fortunately, however, there are other eclipses of antiquity that can be examined — and these are definitely eclipses. Many of these, however, are from the decades and centuries preceding the birth of Christ, and they only rarely give the exact location from which the event was visible. Furthermore, since B.C. chronology is even less secure than A.D., the use of such data is of doubtful value. However, a small number of eclipses are reported from Rome and other locations in the Roman Empire in the first centuries of the Christian era, and since these are often very precise with regard to location and date they have the potential to absolutely confirm or refute both traditional and Illig-based chronologies.

One of the most outstanding of these events is the one reported by Dio Cassius as having occurred in Rome during the funeral of Nero's mother Julia Agrippina, in April A.D. 59. Can this eclipse be confirmed by modern astronomers? It cannot! According to them, retrocalculating solar and lunar positions from our time with the help of advanced computer technology, no eclipse of the sun occurred in Rome in that year — i.e., 1953 years ago. The nearest they can come is a solar eclipse which would have occurred in A.D. 75, but this is far outside any reasonable margin of chronological error. Further, the eclipse of A.D. 75 occurred in January, whereas we know that Nero's mother was buried in April.

Since conventional history thus fails, we must ask: what about Illig; could he perhaps provide an eclipse in Rome at the right time? Assuming that roughly 300 years were added to our calendar during the Middle Ages, we should thus look for an eclipse of the sun in Rome 1653 years ago, in the year designated by astronomers as A.D. 359, according to our calendar. What do the computers show? The answer is clear: According to NASA, a total eclipse of the sun occurred in Rome on March 15, A.D. 359 — almost precisely 300 years after the reported eclipse of A.D. 59!

Consider then the facts: According to Dio Cassius an eclipse of the sun was observed in Rome sometime in the month of April in A.D. 59. He does not name the actual date, though it is believed that Julia Agrippina died in the middle of the March, with most authorities place her death sometime between March 19 and 23. But she was said to have been buried about a month later, in April. Conventional historians argue that no eclipse occurred in Italy during the year 59, or anytime near it. However, assuming that an extra 300 years were added to our calendar during the "Dark Ages," and removing precisely three centuries from it (less 46 days), and bringing us down into the year 1712, we find that an eclipse of the sun would indeed have occurred in March of the year 59 in the city of Rome.

In fact, from the traditionally reported eclipses, 15 deviate (like that of Dio Cassius) by 300 years and 2 by 299 years from retrocalculation. Eleven of these show an exactly identical deviation of 300 years minus 46 days. Here is a tabular representation.

Fig. 8. All Reported Eclipses from the Epoch, with the Amount of Deviation from Retrocalculated Dates:

Source of historical report	Type S|M	Retrocalc. conv. [year C.E.]	Sort, cover	Comments: sort, place of visibility « cons. || alt. »	Retrocalc. alternative	Dev. in Years minus days
Livius III.IX.*	M	21. Jun. -167	T	« Dev. 119 days || 75 days »	06. Mai. 133	+300 -46d
Diodor	S	15. Aug. -309	T	Diodor lived in 1st cy. A.D.	30. Jun. -09	+300 -46d
Julius Obsequens	S	19. Jul. -103	R	Julius O. lived in 4th cy. A.D.	3. Juni 197	+300 -46d
Julius Obsequens	S	29. Jun. -93	R	3 eclipses separated 10 + 30 yrs	14. May 207	+300 -46d
Julius Obsequens	S	-59 ?	X	|| evening »	12. Apr. 237	+300
Augustus' dead	S	18. Apr. 14	V	|| R: Nola/ Naples »	27. Jul. 306	+292 ?
Plinius LIX	S	30. Apr. 59	80%	|| T: Rome »	15. Mar. 359	+300 -46d
Vita Gordianorum	ST	6. Aug. 240	65%	|| T: Rome »	20. Jun. 540	+300 -46d
Cons. Const. 291	S	4. May 292	75%	|| R: Constantinople »	4. Oct. 590	+299
Cons. Const. 318	S	6. May 319	85%	|| R: Constantinople »	4. Nov. 617	+299
Aurelius Victor	S	6. May 319	X	« 317 || R: Pannonia, sunrise »	4. Nov. 617	+300
Pappus of Alexandria	S	18. Oct 320	V	|| T: Constantinople »	5. Oct. 674**	+354 -13d
Theon of Alexandria	S	16. Jun. 364	V	« Baltic (!) || T: Alexand. »	3. Jun. 718**	+354 -13d
Theophanes	S	6. Jun. 346	T	« T: Alexandria || T: C'nople »	5. Nov. 644	+298
Zosimus 6.9.394	S	20. Nov. 393	T	|| 95% at Frigidus »	5. Oct. 693	+300 -46d
Chron Gallorum 418	S	17.Mai. 421	40%	|| T. Rome 80% »	3. Jun. 718	+300
Ann. Lundin. 448	ST	23. Dez. 447	80%	|| T: London »	12. Apr. 758	-310
Hydatius	ST	19. Jul. 418	T	« T: Portugal »	3. Juni 718	+300 -46d

Source of historical report	Type S|M	Retrocalc. conv. [year C.E.]	Sort, cover	Comments: sort, place of visibility «cons. || alt.»	Retrocalc. alternative	Dev. in Years minus days
Hydatius	S	22. Dez. 447	T	|| 70% Portugal »	7. Nov. 747	+300 -46d
Hydatius	M	4. Sep. 451	81%	|| T: »	31. Jul. 752	+301
Hydatius	M	2. Mär. 462	P	|| T: »	4. Jan. 763	+301
Elias Nisibis	S	14. Jan. 484	T	† Peroz after campaign in January?	3. Apr. 786	+302
M. Neapolitanus	ST	14. Jan. 484	U	« invisible in Athens || T: Crete »	3. Apr. 786	-301
Theophanes	ST	29. Jun. 512	T	« T: Crete || T: Athens »	14. May 812	+300 -46d
Bede° 16. Feb 538	S	540 ?	V	|| R: Scotland »	11. Feb 807	+269
Bede° 20. Jun 540	S	20. Jun. 540	V	« T: Rome || R: »	16. July 809	+269
Gregory of Tours °°	S	3. Oct. 563	60%	« Mid VIII.|| R: South. France »	18. Aug. 863	+300 -46d
Gregory of Tours	M	18. Sep. 563	58%	|| 20% 'nec quarta pars' ? »	3. Aug. 863	+300 -46d
Gregory of Tours	M	11. Dez. 577	64%	|| T: 'in nigridinem conv.' »	20. Apr. 878	+301
G. of Tours I.VIII.°°	S	4. Oct. 590	65%	|| R: Central France »	8. Aug. 891	+301

The above evidence is, I would argue, virtually conclusive proof that a full three centuries have been added to our calendar. It is material that needs to be seriously considered by mainstream scholarship. The compiler of the above table, physicist H. E. Korth, admits on his web-page that he had initially been skeptical about Illig's claims. He writes, "Some ten years ago, I read about this 'weird' thesis for the first time." However, instead of dismissing it on the recommendation of establishment scholars, Korth began to investigate the matter for himself: "As a physicist, I began to look for scientific evidence and for a theory, free of conspiracies." The evidence he found, both from astronomy and from the other sciences and disciplines, convinced him that Illig was in fact right.

If only there were more academics like Korth!

If 300 years were added, how do we explain the fifteen retrocalculations which fall outside the 300 year error? To begin with, we need to note that none deviates much from 300 years. Six have 301 years, one has 302 years, and one has 298 years. Only four show any serious deviation: the two reported by Bede (269 years), and those of Pappus of Alexandria and Theon of Alexandria (both 354 years). But as Illig has shown in detail, Bede (who anachronistically uses the zero and the *anno domini* calendar) and everything he says should be treated with the utmost caution. Korth himself has suggested that Bede, writing in the eleventh century (i.e., the eighth), mistook a character of the Merovingian epoch (Chlovis II) with an earlier ruler of that dynasty — which he in fact replicated as the "Carolingian" dynasty — and placed in the time of Louis the Pious. The identical error in the two Alexandrian sources suggest a single scribal mistake.[1] As for the remaining cases (none of which deviates more than a year or two from the normal three centuries), Korth has suggested that these may have been based on a real but locally invisible eclipse that did not match with the new moon (as in the case of Zosimus), or was calculated in accordance with the Byzantine custom of beginning the new year in autumn.

All in all, the fact that the eclipse record of the ancients fits perfectly with astronomical retrocalculation if we assume 300 years need to be subtracted from our calendar is virtually irrefutable proof of Illig's thesis. The chances of such a circumstance being the result of chance are virtually nil.

It is of great importance too, as Korth notes, that astronomical events associated with the life of Christ, which have hitherto been unverifiable, are strikingly confirmed if we assume they occurred 300 years closer to our time. Thus for example the Star of Bethlehem, which Matthew says guided the Wise Men to Jerusalem shortly after Christ's birth, is revealed to be none other than Halley's Comet, which would have presented a spectacular sight in the night skies exactly 1719 years ago (or in A.D. 295, according to the retrocalculated placement of modern astronomers). If Halley's Comet was the Star of Bethlehem, it means that the Wise Men would have arrived in Jerusalem in 5 B.C., which accords well enough with current estimates of Christ's birth date. In fact, since, as Matthew informs us, King Herod ordered the killing of all the male children in Bethlehem two years old or under, "according to the time that he had carefully ascertained from the Magi," (Matthew, 2:16) this would suggest that Christ was born in 7 B.C., or thereabouts.

---

1 The eclipse table can be found on H. E. Korth's website, at www.jahr1000wen.de

As Korth observes, a peculiar feature of Halley's Comet in that year — apart from its unusual brightness — was that it would have, when viewed from Babylonia, appeared to have "stood still" in the western skies (over the land of Israel) for about a month.[1] Korth also notes the fact that as early as 1907 Russian mathematician Nikolai Morosov had placed all the astronomical events of the New Testament — particularly those which seem to be alluded to in John's Apocalypse — in the fourth century. Morosov, not suspecting an error in *Anno Domini* chronology, therefore declared Christianity to be an invention of the fourth century.[2]

Taking everything into consideration I feel we are justified in concurring with Korth's evaluation of the facts: "A coming together of similar events at any other time can certainly be excluded."[3] The astronomical evidence, I feel, shows fairly conclusively that a full three centuries has been added to our chronology, and that the date of publication of this volume, for example, is not 2014 but 1714.

RADIOCARBON DATING AND DENDROCHRONOLOGY

The conventional scheme of history criticized in the present work is not without its own scientific support, or so it is said. Within the past sixty years two new and apparently thoroughly objective dating methods, radiocarbon analysis and dendrochronology, or tree-ring dating, have added their own weight to the historical debate. These have tended to vindicate accepted chronology. Certainly radiocarbon dates for the Roman period are regularly published in scientific journals, and these are almost always broadly in line with chronology as it is familiar to us.

Notwithstanding the confidence with which radiocarbon and dendrochronological dates are quoted in textbooks and the popular media, the limitations of both techniques have been highlighted by numerous authors over the past two or three of decades; though such criticisms tend to be ignored, with the result that the general public is mostly unaware of any problem. This being the case, I shall look briefly in the following pages at some of the more pressing problems. Before going a step further, however, it needs to be stated that, even were radiocarbon an accurate and reliable dating method,

---

1 Korth, op cit., pp. 303-4
2 Nikolai Morosov, *Die Offenbarung Johannis – eine astronomisch-historische Untersuchung* (Stuttgart, 1912)
3 Korth, op. cit., p. 316

it is extremely unlikely that it could ever be used to successfully mount a challenge to the accepted chronology. Only three hundred years are at issue, and this is not a span great enough to cause any major rethink. Thus it would be conceivable that an artifact which looked like it might belong to the first century could be dated, on radiocarbon grounds, to the fourth; and historians would then be content to assume that they made a mistake in originally attributing it to the first century. Perhaps it was a fourth century artifact manufactured in a retro style. So, even if radiocarbon produced accurate results, we should not expect it to be causing major upsets within the scholarly community.

But the fact is, radiocarbon analysis does not produce accurate results and it is not a reliable dating method.

The discovery by Professor Willard Libby of the University of Chicago in 1946 that living organisms absorb a radioactive carbon isotope (carbon 14) from the atmosphere was quickly recognized as a potentially valuable new tool in the archaeologist's repertoire. As soon as a living organism dies, it ceases to absorb carbon 14; from then on the proportion of radioactive carbon in the organism's body begins to decline. Since this decline or "decay" occurs at a fixed rate, it is held that we can determine with great accuracy the age of any artifact containing once-living organic material. The less carbon 14 in a sample, the older it must be.

Archaeologists were quick to avail themselves of the revolutionary new technique, and samples from ancient sites throughout Europe and the Middle East were soon being subjected to analysis. Whilst the results obtained were not always consistent — indeed some were wildly inconsistent — enough information was apparently gathered to convince scholars that the accepted dates for the very ancient civilizations of the Middle East, as well as for the Neolithic and Bronze Ages of Europe, were broadly correct. Academics were less interested in putting Roman material to the test, since the dates given for Roman civilization were never questioned. When Roman age artifacts have been examined, it has been primarily to identify precisely what period of the Roman Age they belong to.

None of the vast number of published radiocarbon results obtained over the past half century, however, has seemed to diverge in any fundamental way from preconceived notions of ancient chronology; and so great is the prestige of "hard science" in our culture that few people have dared to even question these results. Nevertheless, in many other fields, scientific conclusions are regularly questioned, and frequently overturned. This is particularly the case with regard to medical and dietary science, as well as forensic science applied to criminal investigation.

As a matter of fact, the radiocarbon system of dating is well-known by those in the field to have a number of major drawbacks.[1] For one thing, samples can be contaminated, and it is virtually impossible to know that they have been. Contamination comes in many forms, and can either increase or decrease the readings, making the sample under investigation appear either much younger or much older than it is. The most simple, yet possibly most pervasive form of contamination is that of water. Water can literally wash the radioactivity out of a sample, making it look older. There is absolutely no way of knowing whether a control sample has been exposed to water. Now even in Egypt and Mesopotamia few artifacts have never been exposed to water, either from the flooding great rivers of these lands, or from flash-floods caused by admittedly fairly infrequent rainfalls. Just how much water contamination can affect radiocarbon results was dramatically illustrated in a recent *Horizon* documentary screened by the BBC.[2] An Englishman who, in a fit of remorse, had confessed to murdering and dismembering his wife brought police to the spot where he had buried her head. Sure enough, the detectives soon uncovered the partial skull of a woman, complete with some still surviving fleshy tissue. They were astonished when scientists from the British Museum, who had not been informed of the skull's provenance, radiocarbon dated it and declared it to be 1,500 years old. Other forensic scientists, who reconstructed the woman's features, declared that in their opinion the body was indeed that of the vanished wife. The documentary concluded by offering the opinion that bodies found in boggy conditions take on the date of the sodden earth wherein they are interred. In short, the water had leeched much of the carbon isotope from the remains, making it appear vastly older than it was. A major plank in the radiocarbon edifice, the constancy of rates of day, is therefore demolished.

Given this remarkable fact, which in any case has always been well understood by the scholarly community, we may well wonder how esteemed academics can then propose to use radiocarbon readings of samples of wood, leather and bone recovered from the ground that have endured millennia

---

1 See for example *New Scientist* (September, 1989), p.26, where it is noted that the margin of error quoted by some laboratories in their dating techniques may be two or three times greater than admitted. Whilst some laboratories, it is claimed, are consistently correct, others have been shown to produce dates that are up to 250 years out. Unforeseen errors, it is said, can arise in the chemical pre-treatment of small amounts of material, and dates can be way out on samples only 200 years old.

2 BBC 2 *Horizon*, 4th March 1999

of rainfalls and river floods? Yet such readings are still regularly published, without comment.

With wood there is an added complication. A tree can live for hundreds of years, but at any given time only absorbs radioactive carbon into its outermost layer. Thus it is necessary to know the age of the tree when it was cut down, as well as the part of the tree from which the timber was derived, before we can even begin to talk about an accurate reading. Yet once again, timber is indiscriminately dated by scientists and the results published without comment.

A third — and major — problem is the tendency of scientists to dismiss anomalous results that do not conform to preconceived ideas. Thus a very substantial number of results obtained from Egypt and Mesopotamia have produced startlingly recent figures; yet these have not been published, or have at best been reduced to footnotes, because, ironically enough, the researchers have deemed them to be "contaminated". In the words of one eminent scholar:

> "Some archaeologists refused to accept radiocarbon dates. The attitude probably, in the early days of the new technique, was summed up by Professor Jo Brew, Director of the Peabody Museum at Harvard, "If a C14 date supports our theories, we put it in the main text. If it does not entirely contradict them, we put it in the footnote. And if it is completely 'out of date,' we just drop it."[1]

Perhaps the greatest problem with regard to radiocarbon dating is the question of environment. All researchers in the field assume that environmental conditions have more or less always been as they now are; at least as far back as humanity's first appearance on the planet. Yet during periods of catastrophic disturbances in nature, such as those caused by volcanic eruptions and conflagrations, much "old" carbon (i.e., carbon with a depleted proportion of carbon 14) would be released into the atmosphere — to then be absorbed by living organisms. In such circumstances plants and animals would have a much lower percentage of radioactive carbon in their systems than present day organisms. The well-known eruption of Vesuvius in A.D.

---

1 David Wilson *The New Archaeology* (New York, 1974), p. 97. An example of this pernicious practice is seen in the fate of samples from the tomb of pharaoh Tutankhamun subjected by the British Museum to the radio-carbon method. The samples, consisting of fibres of a reed mat and a palm kernel, produced dates of 844 BC and 899 BC respectively. These were broadly in line with the date for Tutankhamun predicted by Velikovsky, but were roughly 500 years too recent for textbook chronology. In spite of assurances given to Velikovsky, the dates were never formally published. See Velikovsky's *Peoples of the Sea* (1977), p.xvi

79, which destroyed the cities of Herculaneum and Pompeii, would likely have produced major fluctuations in the composition of atmospheric carbon.

This is a well-documented problem, and is termed the "Suess effect" in honor of the scientist who first identified it. Its impact is not theoretical, but proven. In this way it was demonstrated, for example, how the massive use of fossil fuels in the twentieth century (with their attendant release of great amounts of "old" carbon) led to some startlingly anomalous results: "We are told that plants in a rich old carbon environment were radiocarbon dated several thousand years older than they actually were, and a tree by an airport was actually dated to be 10,000 years old."[1]

Thus another major plank of the radiocarbon edifice, the constancy of initial conditions (as well as rates of decay), collapses.

But there is another scientific dating method widely touted as a reliable guide to ancient chronology: dendrochronology.

***

The idea that tree rings could supply an accurate record of the climate dating back many centuries has been around for some time. The rings of any felled tree tell, at a glance, which years were cold and which were warm. Warm summers of course produce more growth and therefore a thicker ring. Whilst an individual tree, such as an oak, may live many centuries, its lifespan is still finite. However, during the 19 s it was suggested that since patterns of rings are quite specific to the climate of a particular locality (e.g., the rings may show that in the first decade of the eighteenth century in Ireland two warm years were followed by four cold years which were followed by five warm years etc.), it might be possible to construct a tabular record of the climate far beyond the lifespan of any individual tree. And so, for example, the central rings of a 500-year-old oak would have a specific pattern of warm and cold summers which could be compared with patterns on old artifacts made of oak trees which had been felled just short of 500 years ago. In this way, the ring pattern at the core of the newly felled oak should match the ring pattern at the outside of the tree felled 500 years ago.

Over the past forty years great efforts have been made, particularly in a number of European universities, to thus construct a climate record going back many centuries. Dendrochronologists working at Queen's University in Belfast claim to have established just such a climate record going back

---

1 Charles Ginenthal "The Extinction of the Mammoth" *The Velikovskian* (special edition) Vol.III 2 and 3 (1999), p.184

7,000 years, whilst other tree-ring schools claim counts as high as 8,200 years. If these records are accurate they could potentially provide archaeologists with a valuable tool. So for example an article made of wood, from an archaeological find of known date, could have that date either verified or refuted by the tree ring pattern in the wood. And sure enough, a number of such computations have been made; and they all, surprise, surprise, confirm existing chronologies.

As I have said, I do not want to go into the dendrochronology debate in detail, since a proper critique would fill a volume on its own. As with the radiocarbon method, tree ring dating has tended to be used only to pinpoint precisely where an artifact belongs within the existing scheme of things. This is because the chronology of the Roman world is not doubted or even remotely questioned. An artifact which looks like it might belong to the first century may be dated, on radiocarbon or dendrochronological grounds, to the fourth; and historians are then content to assume that they made a mistake in originally attributing it to the first century. Yet far more frequently the dendrochronological result somehow fits neatly into the preconceived time-frame. This is because, as with radiocarbon, the archaeologists tend — one way or another — to get the results they expect.

In fact, dendrochronology cannot properly be called an exact science; there are far too many unknowns involved. For example, we must be sure that all the wood being compared is from trees from the same climate area. This in itself is almost impossible to prove. Secondly, how do we define a climate area? Even regions fairly close can have very differing climates; and in the past may have differed even more. No one really knows. In addition, although the climate record in any given area might be unique over a long period, it is almost certainly not unique over a short period. Thus, many regions of the world could have three warm summers followed by four cold ones followed by two warm ones. For a pattern to be really significant, we need a much longer unbroken record. Yet many historical artifacts made of wood provide us with a record of only ten or twenty years or even less. And one other problem cannot be ignored: as we go further into the past, artifacts of all kinds, but especially those made of wood and other perishable materials, become much scarcer. From really ancient times, we are lucky to get enough wood to establish a pattern of more than five or six years. Such a scanty record cannot be used with confidence.

All of this makes it highly likely that the carefully constructed tree ring record stretching back to antiquity, so proudly advertised by the European universities, is a force fit and therefore a fake — and completely useless to the historian. And in fact more than one dendrochronologist has admitted that many tree-ring patterns have to be force fit in order to produce a lengthy chronology. Consider for example what M. A. Stokes and T. L. Smiley have to say: "[W]hile several of the patterns match, there are many individual rings which do not match from plot to plot. This variation is typical. It is logical to ask how many unmatched rings can be accepted in what we call matched plots. Our answer would have to be that, when most of the rings match, the fit is considered correct. While this may sound like a very unscientific answer, the experienced dendrochronologists using these methods are able to duplicate each other."[1] Another well-known dendrochronologist, M. G. L. Baillie, acknowledged another important weakness in tree-ring dating: "It is very easy to make the results seem excessively tidy. This is usually the result of attempting to present the results in too logical a fashion. The fact of the matter is that dendrochronological research is not all that logical in itself, it is only logical with hindsight.... Here the 'art' of dendrochronology becomes apparent."[2]

In light of all this, the very least we can say is that dendrochronology is an inexact science and its findings open to interpretation. It cannot, and should not, be regarded as providing a definitive judgment on the chronology of the ancient world.

---

1 M. A. Stokes and T. L. Smiley, *An Introduction to Tree-Ring Dating* (University of Chicago Press, 1968), p. 50
2 M. G. L. Baillie, *Tree-Ring Dating and Archaeology* (University of Chicago Press, 1982), p. 23

Bibliography

Atroshenko, V. I. and Judith Collins, *The Origins of the Romanesque* (Lund Humphries, London, 1985)

Baillie, M. G. L., *Tree-Ring Dating and Archaeology* (University of Chicago Press, 1982)

Bertrand, Louis and Sir Charles Petrie, *The History of Spain* (2nd ed., London, 1945)

Bowerstock, Glen W., "The Vanishing Paradigm of the Fall of Rome," *Bulletin of the American Academy of Arts and Sciences*, Vol. 49, No.8 (May, 1996)

Brown, Peter, *The Making of Late Antiquity* (Harvard University Press, 1978)

Campbell, James, *The Anglo-Saxons* (Harmondsworth, London, 1982)

Clarke, H. and B. Ambrosiani, *Towns in the Viking Age* (St. Martin's Press, New York, 1995)

Collins, Roger, *Early Medieval Spain: Unity in Diversity, 400–1000*, (2nd ed. Macmillan, 1995)

Collins, Roger, *Spain: An Oxford Archaeological Guide* (Oxford University Press, 1998)

Creswell, K. A. C., *A Short Account of Early Muslim Architecture* Vol. 2 (Scolar Press, London, 1968)

Crone, Patricia and Michael Cook, *Hagarism: The Making of the Islamic World* (Cambridge University Press, 1977)

Dark, Ken., *Britain and the End of the Roman Empire* (Stroud, 2001)

Dunand, M., *Fouilles de Byblos I*, (Paul Geuthner, Paris, 1939); and N. Jidejian. *Byblos through the Ages*, (Beirut, 1971)

Folz, Robert, *The Coronation of Charlemagne* (Routledge and Kegan Paul, London, 1974) (English translation of *Le couronnement impérial de Charlemagne*, 1964)

Geary, Patrick J., *Before France and Germany: The Creation and Transformation of the Merovingian World* (Oxford University Press, 1988)

Ginenthal, Charles, "The Extinction of the Mammoth" *The Velikovskian* (special edition) Vol.III 2 and 3 (1999)

Grant, Edward, *God and Reason in the Middle Ages* (Cambridge University Press, 2001)

Guillaume, Alfred, "The Version of the Gospels Used in Medina Circa 700 AD." *Al-Andalus* 15 (1950)

Hårdh, B. and L. Larsson, (eds.), *Central Places in the Migration and Merovingian Periods* (Department of Archaeology and Ancient History, Lund, 2002)

Harris, William V., "Child Exposure in the Roman Empire," *The Journal of Roman Studies*, Vol. 84 (1994)

Hay, Denys, *Annalists and Historians: Western Historiography from the VII to the XVII Centuries* (Metheun, London, 1977)

Heinsohn, Gunnar, "The Gaonic Period in the Land of Israel/Palestine," *Society for Interdisciplinary Studies; Chronology and Catastrophism Review*, No. 2 (2002)

Herzfeld, Ernst, *Ausgrabungen von Samarra VI. Geschichte der Stadt Samarra* (Berlin, 1948)

Hodges, Richard and David Whitehouse, *Mohammed, Charlemagne and the Origins of Europe* (London, 1982)

Hubert, Jean, *L'Art Préroman* (Paris, 1938)

Illig, Heribert, "Calendar Reforms of Caesar and Gregory XIII," *Society for Interdisciplinary Studies: Chronology and Catastrophism Review*, (2001)

Illig, Heribert, *Das erfundene Mittelalter* (Ullstein, Berlin, 2005)

Illig, Heribert, *Wer hat an der Uhr gedreht?* (Econ Taschenbuch Verlag, 2000)

Jaki, Stanley L., "Medieval Creativity in Science and Technology," in *Patterns and Principles and Other Essays* (Intercollegiate Studies Institute, Bryn Mawr, Pennsylvania, 1995)

James, Edward, *The Franks* (Basil Blackwell, Oxford, 1988)

Janssen, Walter, "The rebirth of towns in the Rhineland," in Richard Hodges and Brian Hobley (eds.) *The Rebirth of Towns in the West, AD 750 to 1050* (Council for British Archaeology, 1988)

Jeffery, Arthur, *The Foreign Vocabulary of the Qur'an* (Oriental Institute Baroda, Vadodara, India, 1938)

Korpås, Ola, Per Wideström and Jonas Ström, "The recently found hoards from Spillings farm on Gotland, Sweden," *Viking Heritage Magazine*, 4 (2000)

Korth, Hans-Erdmann, *Der Grösste Irrtum der Weltgeschichte* (Engelsdorfer Verlag, Leipzig, 2013)

Lackner, H., "Multikulti in Ur-Wien. Archäologie. Historiker schreiben die Geschichte Wiens neu: Anders als bisher angenommen, war die Stadt zu Beginn des Mittelalters 300 Jahre lang eine menschenleere Ruinenlandschaft," in *Profil*, Vienna (2010)

Lings, Martin, *Muhammad: His Life Based on the Earliest Sources* (Inner Traditions, 2006)

Livermore, Harold V., *The Origins of Spain and Portugal* (George Allen and Unwin, Ltd., London, 1971)

Luxenberg, Christoph, *The Syro-Aramaic Reading of the Koran: A Contribution to the Decoding of the Language of the Koran* (Prometheus Books, 2007)

Mango, Cyril, *Byzantium: The Empire of New Rome* (Orion Books, 2005)

Montalembert, Charles, *The Monks of the West: From St. Benedict to St. Bernard.* Vol. 5, (London, 1896)

Morosov, Nikolai, *Die Offenbarung Johannis–eine astronomisch-historische Untersuchung* (Stuttgart, 1912)

Moss, H. St. L. B., *The Birth of the Middle Ages; 395-814* (Oxford University Press, 1935)

Murphey, Rhoads, "The Decline of North Africa since the Roman Occupation: Climatic or Human?" *ANNALS, Association of American Geographers*, Vol. XLI, no. 2, (June, 1951)

Naphtali, Lewis, (ed.) "Papyrus Oxyrhynchus 744," *Life in Egypt Under Roman Rule* (Oxford University Press, 1985)

Newman, John Henry, in Charles Frederick Harrold, (ed.) *Essays and Sketches*, Vol. 3 (New York, 1948)

Niemitz, Hans-Ulrich, "Archäologie und Kontinuität. Gab es Städte zwischen Spätantike und Mittelalter?" *Zeitensprünge* IV (1992, No. 3)

Ohlig Karl-Heinz and Gerd-R Puin (eds.) *The Hidden Origins of Islam: New Research into its Early History* (Prometheus Books, 2009)

Painter, Sidney, *A History of the Middle Ages, 284-1500* (Macmillan, New York, 1953)

Pines, Shlomo, *The Jewish Christians Of The Early Centuries Of Christianity According To A New Source.* Proceedings of the Israel Academy of Sciences and Humanities II, No. 13 (1966)

Pressburg, Norbert, *Good Bye Mohammed: Wie der Islam wirklich entstand* (2009)

Retso, Jan, *The Arabs in Antiquity: Their History from the Assyrians to the Umayyads* (Rutledge and Kegan Paul, London, 2003)

Riley-Smith, Jonathan, "The State of Mind of Crusaders to the East: 1095-1300," in Jonathan Riley-Smith (ed.) *Oxford History of the Crusades*, (Oxford University Press, 2002)

Rogers, J. M., "Samarra: a study in medieval town planning," in A. Hourani and S. M. Stern (eds.), *The Islamic City* (Oxford University Press, 1970).

Russell, Jeffrey Burton, *Inventing the Flat Earth: Columbus and Modern Historians* (Praeger Publications, 1991)

Ryckmans, Jan, "La chronologie des rois de Saba et Du-Raydan," *Journal of the Netherlands Institute for the Near East*, Vol. 16 (1964)

Sambursky, Samuel, *The Physical World of Late Antiquity* (Routledge and Kegan Paul, 1962

Schultz, Gwen, *Ice Age Lost* (New York, 1974)

Schulz, Mattias, "Schwindel im Skriptorium. Reliquienkult, erfundene Märtyrer, gefälschte Kaiserurkunden–phantasievolle Kleriker haben im Mittelalter ein gigantisches Betrugswerk in Szene gesetzt. Neuester Forschungsstand: Über

60 Prozent aller Königsdokumente aus der Merowingerzeit wurden von Mönchen getürkt," *Der Spiegel*, 29 (1998)

Spencer, Robert, *Did Muhammad Exist? An Enquiry into Islam's Obscure Origins* (ISI Books, Delaware, 2012).

Stark, Rodney, *The Rise of Christianity: A Sociologist Reconsiders History* (Harper Collins, 1996)

Stenton, Frank, *Anglo-Saxon England* (3rd ed., Oxford, 1973)

Stokes, M. A. and T. L. Smiley, *An Introduction to Tree-Ring Dating* (University of Chicago Press, 1968)

Thacker, A. T., "Early medieval Chester: the historical background," in Richard Hodges and Brian Hobley (eds.) *The Rebirth of Towns in the West, AD 750 to 1050* (Council for British Archaeology, 1988)

Thompson, E. A., "The Barbarian Kingdoms in Gaul and Spain," *Nottingham Mediaeval Studies*, 7 (1963)

Trevor-Roper, Hugh, *The Rise of Christian Europe* (2nd. ed., London, 1966)

Verwers, W. J. H., "Dorestad: a Carolingian town?" in Richard Hodges and Brian Hobley (eds.) *The Rebirth of Towns in the West, AD 750 to 1050* (Council for British Archaeology, 1988)

Ward-Perkins, Bryan, *The Fall of Rome and the End of Civilization* (Oxford University Press, 2006)

Wells, Peter, *Barbarians to Angels* (W. W. Norton and Co., New York, 2008)

Whitehouse, David, *Siraf III. The Congregational Mosque* (London, British Institute of Persian Studies, 1980)

Wickham, Chris., *The Inheritance of Rome: Illuminating the Dark Ages 400–1000* (Penguin Books, 2009)

Index